T0332471

SYNCHRONIZATION IN
REAL-TIME SYSTEMS
A Priority Inheritance Approach

THE KLUWER INTERNATIONAL SERIES
IN ENGINEERING AND COMPUTER SCIENCE

REAL-TIME SYSTEMS

Consulting Editor

John A. Stankovic

REAL-TIME UNIX SYSTEMS: *Design and Application Guide,*
B. Furht, D. Grostick, D. Gluch, G. Rabbat, J. Parker, M. McRoberts,
ISBN: 0-7923-9099-7

FOUNDATIONS OF REAL-TIME COMPUTING: *Scheduling and Resource Management,* A. M. van Tilborg, G. M. Koob
ISBN: 0-7923-9166-7

FOUNDATIONS OF REAL-TIME COMPUTING: *Formal Specifications and Methods,* A. M. van Tilborg,
ISBN: 0-7923-9167-5

CONSTRUCTING PREDICTABLE REAL TIME SYSTEMS,
W. A. Halang, A. D. Stoyenko
ISBN: 0-7923-9202-7

SYNCHRONIZATION IN REAL-TIME SYSTEMS
A Priority Inheritance Approach

by

Ragunathan Rajkumar
IBM, Thomas J. Watson Research Center

KLUWER ACADEMIC PUBLISHERS
Boston/Dordrecht/London

Distributors for North America:
Kluwer Academic Publishers
101 Philip Drive
Assinippi Park
Norwell, Massachusetts 02061 USA

Distributors for all other countries:
Kluwer Academic Publishers Group
Distribution Centre
Post Office Box 322
3300 AH Dordrecht, THE NETHERLANDS

Library of Congress Cataloging-in-Publication Data

Rajkumar, Ragunathan.
    Synchronization in real-time systems : a priority inheritance
approach / by Ragunathan Rajkumar.
      p.   cm. -- (The Kluwer international series in engineering and
computer science ; 151. Real-time systems)
    Includes bibliographical references and index.
    ISBN 0-7923-9211-6
    1. Real-time data processing.   I. Title.   II. Series: Kluwer
international series in engineering and computer science ; SECS
151.   III. Series: Kluwer international series in engineering and
computer science. Real-time systems.
QA76.54.R35   1991
004'.33--dc20   91-24711
                                                    CIP

Copyright © 1991 by Kluwer Academic Publishers

All rights reserved. No part of this publication may be reproduced, stored in a retrieval
system or transmitted in any form or by any means, mechanical, photo-copying, recording,
or otherwise, without the prior written permission of the publisher, Kluwer Academic
Publishers, 101 Philip Drive, Assinippi Park, Norwell, Massachusetts 02061.

Printed on acid-free paper.

Printed in the United States of America

To my Parents

Table of Contents

List of Figures

List of Tables

Preface

Real-time computing systems are vital to a wide range of applications. For example, they are used in the control of nuclear reactors and automated manufacturing facilities, in controlling and tracking air traffic, and in communication systems. In recent years, real-time systems have also grown larger and become more critical. For instance, advanced aircraft such as the space shuttle must depend heavily on computer systems [Carlow 84]. The centralized control of manufacturing facilities and assembly plants operated by robots are other examples at the heart of which lie embedded real-time systems. Military defense systems deployed in the air, on the ocean surface, land and underwater, have also been increasingly relying upon real-time systems for monitoring and operational safety purposes, and for retaliatory and containment measures. In telecommunications and in multi-media applications, real-time characteristics are essential to maintain the integrity of transmitted data, audio and video signals.

Many of these systems control, monitor or perform critical operations, and must respond quickly to emergency events in a wide range of embedded applications. They are therefore required to process tasks with stringent timing requirements and must perform these tasks in a way that these timing requirements are guaranteed to be met. Real-time scheduling algorithms attempt to ensure that system timing behavior meets its specifications, but typically assume that tasks do not share logical or physical resources. Since resource-sharing cannot be eliminated, synchronization primitives must be used to ensure that resource consistency constraints are not violated. Unfortunately, existing mechanisms for achieving task synchronization can lead to uncontrolled priority inversion, a situation in which a higher priority job is blocked by lower priority jobs for an indefinite period of time. Unless the priority inversion problem is addressed adequately, scheduling algorithms can be of little use in real-time systems.

Goals of This Book

This book studies the principles of task synchronization in real-time systems by investigating the impact of synchronization delays on timing constraints. It develops a comprehensive set of techniques for synchronizing real-time tasks on uniprocessors, shared memory multiprocessors, distributed systems and distributed real-time databases. In particular, we investigate the class of *priority inheritance protocols* that solve the unbounded blocking problem, which is a generalization of the priority inversion problem. We show that there exist *efficient* priority inheritance protocols on uniprocessors. Since synchronization is essentially a serializing activity, the durations of blocking on shared resources become prolonged in the context of multiprocessors and distributed systems. We develop priority inheritance protocols for use on multiprocessors and distributed systems which bound the blocking duration of a task waiting for globally shared resources. We also extend the priority inheritance protocols to distinguish between the read and write semantics of locks in real-time databases. We show that compatible locks are not necessarily useful in real-time databases, but our protocol shall exploit such lock compatibility when it enhances guaranteed performance. This protocol can be extended to decomposable distributed real-time databases as well.

Our primary focus in this book is upon the delay introduced by the sharing of resources. The intended goal is to bound this delay, reduce it as much as possible and account for it in the scheduling analysis. However, it is important to note that bounding the delay caused by task synchronization is not an end in itself. First and foremost, the system must be amenable to scheduling analysis in the absence of resource-sharing. The bounded delay due to resource-sharing serves only to approximate the idealized independent task scheduling model, with the net effect of making the real-time system predictable.

Acknowledgments

Without the help and support of several people at Carnegie Mellon University, IBM Research and elsewhere, this book would not have become possible.

If I now believe that I am capable of doing some research, I owe it to Dr. Lui Sha, my mentor, who introduced me to the intriguing domain of research, and taught me to question basic assumptions. Discussions, technical and otherwise, that I have had with him have always been rewarding. Thank you for everything, Lui. My eternal gratitude is also due Prof. John Lehoczky, for his incisive questioning every step of the way. His deep insight and ability to formulate research problems have never failed to amaze me. In fact, much of the work presented in this book was done with Dr. Sha and Prof. Lehoczky. My sincere thanks to Prof. Jay Strosnider, an office-mate at first, a friend then and my advisor finally! It was a pleasure to bounce ideas off him, and his amicable personality made my stay at CMU all the more enjoyable. I am grateful to Prof. Dan Siewiorek for adopting me as his student under (my) difficult circumstances, and for all the pieces of advice he has given me before and after graduation. Finally, I sincerely thank my manager at IBM Research, Dr. Robert Iannucci, and the IBM Research management who let me steal time away from my work to do this book.

I also thank the Advanced Real-time Technology (ART) project members at CMU for creating the wonderful environment where work was fun. In particular, I thank Dr. Hide Tokuda, Brinkley Sprunt, Dave Kirk, Tom Marchok and especially Joan Maddamma. Dr. Andre van Tilborg was instrumental in getting me into this group. Technical discussions at the Software Engineering Institute with the RTSIA'ns Dr. John Goodenough, Mark Borger, Mark Klein, Bob Page and Tom Ralya were always very informative. Prof. Krithi Ramamritham presented the synchronization protocol on shared memory multiprocessors at the Distributed Systems Conference on my behalf, and contributed to the development of the Semaphore Control Protocol. Mark Borger implemented the uniprocessor protocols on an Ada run-time system for a 68K-target and collected the test data. Mark Klein and Mark Borger pointed out that the deadline avoidance property of the priority ceiling protocol is superior to that of the ceiling semaphore protocol.

The B52's (Tom Marchok, Ron Mraz, CJ Paul and Brinkley Sprunt) deserve special mention for the light-hearted office atmosphere. I also thank Bala Kumar, Gandhi Chinnadurai, Salemites, and the CMU and Pittsburgh folks who contributed more than I can acknowledge. But for my wonderful undergraduate years at PSG Tech, I would be a very different person now and none of this would have ever happened. My thanks to the entire batch of '79-'84 and in particular to all my ECE-mates.

I am extremely grateful for the love, understanding, support and extreme patience shown all along by my wife Revathi. She taught me that life is much more than working at a dumb terminal. And my love goes to Vikram, for all his smiles, playfulness and curiosity. Without him being born, this book would have been written much sooner. It was certainly worth it! And thanks to my brother Mohan Kumar and sister Roop Kala for everything they had to offer during my many years at and away from home.

Finally, I am grateful to my parents, especially to my late father who built in me the resolve to fight for what I wanted, and to my mother who was always there. Their relentless encouragement was perhaps the single most influential factor in my education since childhood. I dedicate this book to them.

SYNCHRONIZATION IN
REAL-TIME SYSTEMS
A Priority Inheritance Approach

Chapter One

Introduction

"In a real-time system, the right result late is wrong."

1.1 REAL-TIME SYSTEMS

The built-in notion of *time* and how it is used in the system is the basic difference between real-time systems and non-real-time systems. More formally, a real-time system is defined as one in which the correctness of its output(s) depends not only upon the logical computations carried out but also upon the time at which the results are delivered to the external interface. In other words, a real-time computation is considered *wrong* (not just late!) if the results are generated at the wrong time.

Naturally, the next question is how the timeliness of a computation is defined to be part of its correctness. This relationship between timeliness and correctness can take several forms, sometimes within the same system. Consider the following computations:

- A navigation system invokes a function to compute the current position of a ship in motion. However, if the result is not computed within a certain time interval, the computed position is considered to be wrong i.e. beyond the acceptable margin of error. The margin of error that is permissible would be part of the system specification.

- A control system processes a sensor signal that arrives periodically. If any instance of this signal is dropped or not processed completely, an error may be considered to have occurred. This can happen, for instance, if the processing of one instance was not completed before the arrival of the next instance.

- A panic signal in a nuclear reactor or a missile alert signal in a fighter aircraft must be effectively responded to within a specified interval of time. Otherwise, damage to life and/or property may result.

In general, a real-time task falls into one of 3 categories depending upon its arrival pattern and its timing constraint (mostly called a deadline). If a task deadline is critical to system functionality and must be met, it is classified as a *hard deadline*. The third computation above presents 2 examples with hard deadlines, failure to meet which can be potentially catastrophic. In contrast, if it is desirable to meet a deadline but occasional missing of the deadline is tolerable, this deadline is considered to be a *soft deadline*. In the first computation above, for example, a relatively large error in the computation of the ship's position "occasionally" may be tolerated as long as the error does not accumulate. The same applies to the second example. However, from an analytical perspective, it is generally easier to guarantee that a timing constraint will be met all the time than to ensure that at least one of two or more successive deadlines will be met. As a result, periodic computations are typically treated as having hard deadlines. The last category of computation that may be executed in a real-time system is one with *no* specific deadline. Background tasks like maintenance and testing activities typically fall into this category.

A complex real-time system has, in general, both hard and soft deadlines. Since the hard deadlines are critical to the functioning of the system, they must be met even under the worst-case conditions. As a result, the system's performance under the worst-case conditions is fundamental to many, if not all, real-time systems. In contrast, the average-case performance is emphasized in general-purpose systems even at the expense of the worst-case performance. In a similar vein, *latency* (the time between data input and data output) is of primary importance in real-time systems while *throughput* (the total amount of processing) is more emphasized in non-real-time systems.

A distinct characteristic of many real-time systems is that it is normally embedded within a "black box" and satisfies a set of pre-defined specifica-

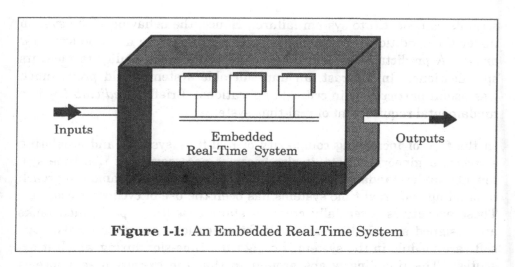

Figure 1-1: An Embedded Real-Time System

tions. This notion is illustrated in Figure 1-1 , where the computing engine comprising the real-time system could be a simple-minded uniprocessor, a shared memory multiprocessor or even a loosely coupled network of computers. The inputs to the system may be taken via sensor devices (e.g. keyboard, control knobs, A/D converters) and the outputs may be delivered to actuators (e.g. relays, displays, plotters, D/A converters, tracking devices). For instance, the external interface of a real-time system controlling a nuclear reactor might consist of a control panel by means of which operators can interactively control the state of the reactor. Such an embedded system, unlike a traditional time-shared system or a batch system, is generally not programmable by the end-user.

Another distinguishing feature of real-time systems is that embedded systems typically either function in an environment which may not permit direct human interaction with the system or operate on a time-scale which is too short for effective human interaction. The Mars Rover [Kanade 90], a self-navigating robot planned for use in the unmanned exploration of the planet Mars, is an example of a real-time system where immediate human interaction is impossible because it takes about 30 minutes for a signal to travel from Earth to Mars. In the US Navy's Inertial Navigation System described by Landherr and Klein [Landherr 89], the position of a ship must be updated every 2.5 milliseconds, a time-frame obviously not very suitable for human intervention.

The inability of an embedded real-time system to meet its timing constraints can constitute system failure. Hence, the behavior of the system under the conditions in which it is expected to operate must be known *a priori*. A predictable system breeds confidence in its ability to meet its specifications. In contrast, an unpredictable system would prove much less useful particularly in critical applications. Briefly, *predictability* is a fundamental requirement of real-time systems.

In the face of increasing complexity of real-time systems and escalating software engineering costs, it also becomes necessary that real-time systems be understandable and modifiable. However, the common approach to building such real-time systems has been the use of cyclical executives. These executives essentially create a static *time-line*, upon which tasks are assigned specific time intervals for execution. In other words, each software module in the system is assigned a time-slot during which it executes. The time-line wraps around so that the execution sequence is repeated over and over again. The time-line is typically handcrafted such that all resource and timing constraints are resolved and must usually be re-done for even modest changes in system requirements. This *ad hoc* approach leads to systems which are very brittle, very difficult to understand, and very expensive to maintain or modify [Softech 86]. Furthermore, since the time-line is static, this approach is not suitable for dynamic requirements such as the need to provide good response to asynchronous requests.

The alternative to the use of *ad hoc* techniques like cyclical executives is the use of algorithmic scheduling techniques, which are built on sound scientific principles. The aim of this approach is to develop theoretical foundations upon which a science of real-time systems can be built. Thus, the intent is to transform the art of crafting real-time systems into a scientific discipline of designing real-time systems. The theoretical underpinnings of this approach attempt to model system timing behavior in mathematical terms. This yields the property of *analyzability*, which while offering predictability, also makes it possible for a designer to hypothesize changes to the system and to evaluate their impact on system timing behavior. The use of scheduling algorithms such as the rate-monotonic algorithm or the earliest deadline algorithm [Liu 73] falls into this category.

Real-time systems typically process multiple signals in order to accomplish different aspects of the system functionality. For instance, an avionics system [Locke 90] computes or controls multiple functions, such as computation of the plane's attitude, sensor control, actuator release, radar control, steering control and built-in testing. Each of these aspects being controlled may have its own timing constraints and can be accomplished by a separate task. However, there is a sizable amount of data that is shared between one or more of these tasks. In order to maintain the consistency and integrity of the shared data, the tasks must synchronize their accesses to the data. Else, the validity of the data and the system's capability to meet its specifications can be compromised.

1.2 SCHEDULING IN REAL-TIME SYSTEMS

Multiple tasks must be scheduled on a finite set of hardware resources in both traditional multiprogramming systems and in real-time systems. It is therefore important to distinguish the objectives of real-time scheduling theory from the goals usually considered in scheduling problems in time-shared systems or in various branches of Operations Research, such as queueing theory or job shop scheduling theory [Stankovic 88]. In time-shared systems, the figures of merit are generally total system throughput and the average response time. However, tasks do not have any critical timing constraints, and an unknown delay in the delivery of results is deemed acceptable. In contrast, real-time systems require analyzable and predictable behavior in terms of guaranteed deadlines and predicted response time for each class of events. High throughput is desired in real-time systems but *not* at the expense of predictability.

Another concept underlying time-shared systems is the notion of *fairness*. For example, when two or more tasks are waiting to obtain the lock on a shared resource, they would be allocated the resource on a first-come-first-served basis. The idea is to avoid potential starvation of some tasks. However, in real-time systems, fairness is of little concern. As long as the timing constraints of tasks are met, tasks should be scheduled so as to increase resource utilization. However, when deadlines have to be missed, a fairness doctrine should not be adhered to, and critical tasks should be scheduled to meet their deadlines even at the expense of less critical tasks.

In most scheduling problems in operations research, one begins with a fixed system of service sites with specified service characteristics. The throughput and average response time is then computed for certain well-specified arrival processes. One attempts to identify system bottlenecks and improve the speed of service offered at those sites. Much of queueing network theory is performed under assumptions which allow the network to be decomposed into independent parts. Moreover, this theory does not typically address the problem of ensuring that real-time tasks meet hard deadlines. Thus, in non-real-time system scheduling, the focus is typically on the autonomy of subsystems and the average task performance, while in real-time systems the focus is on the coordination of sub-systems and on the satisfaction of individual task timing requirements.

In real-time systems, time is central to the correctness of the computations, and the timeliness of each task completion assumes great significance. As a result, well-understood algorithms must be used to allocate time to tasks causing scheduling theory to be a key scientific discipline in building predictable real-time systems. Scheduling theory for real-time systems deals with the quantitative study of the timing behavior of these systems and the development of scheduling algorithms to meet their timing requirements. The objective of this theory is to schedule all system resources using algorithms whose behavior is well-understood. This approach causes the timing behavior of a real-time system to be not only predictable but also analyzable. It then becomes possible to abstract away the finer details of the implementation and to deal with system timing behavior at higher levels of abstraction. For instance, a basic measure of the scheduling algorithm that we use is the processor utilization level below which the deadlines of all tasks can be met [Lehoczky 89, Liu 73]. Thus, software can be freely modified as long as the total utilization of the tasks is held within this limit.

Another key feature of real-time scheduling algorithms is that a task priority as assigned by a scheduling algorithm need not necessarily correspond to the criticality of the task. For instance, the rate-monotonic scheduling algorithm assigns priorities based on the periodicity of a task. In specific, a task with a shorter period is assigned a higher priority. However, a task with a shorter period need not necessarily be more semantically important to the mission than a task with a longer period. In other words, the *scheduling priority* of a task may not be identical to its *semantic importance*. However, the distinction is of no concern when all tasks in the system meet their deadlines. In several real-time systems, a transient overload might develop, and it may not be possible to meet all deadlines under such conditions. When such an overload develops, it becomes imperative that the critical tasks in the system meet their deadlines even at the cost of less critical deadlines. Thus, the notion of task criticality is relevant only when an overload develops and some deadlines *must* be missed. In the case of the rate-monotonic scheduling algorithm, a technique known as *period transformation* [Sha 86] can be used to guarantee that critical tasks will still meet their deadlines when an overload develops.

Problems in real-time scheduling span a wide range of issues. One must specify the characteristics of the real-time tasks being executed by the system. Tasks can be *periodic, sporadic* or *aperiodic* in nature [Mok 83]. Periodic tasks are those which have to be processed at regular intervals, and each instance of a periodic task must be normally completed before the next instance of the same task arrives. Sporadic tasks are asynchronous tasks that may have "hard" deadlines which must be met, but have a minimum interarrival duration between instances. Aperiodic tasks arrive at irregular intervals but have only soft deadlines. In other words, the deadlines for the aperiodic tasks is not rigid, but a good response time is typically desirable. Thus, task timing requirements may be represented by a hard deadline or a response time requirement. Each task may also be assigned a value function [Locke 85] giving the worth of completing a particular task at a particular time.

Tasks also have resource requirements (e.g. processors, I/O channels, communication media or secondary storage), and execution times which can be either deterministic or stochastic. Real-time tasks may have a semantic importance under the particular system *mode* in operation. For example, an avionics system may run one set of tasks during takeoff, another in cruise mode, and yet another during landing. A task may have a different criticality in each of these three modes. Finally, tasks may be independent or have mutual exclusion requirements, i.e. they may share data and resources, or may need to synchronize with each other. In other words, a task inside a critical section accessing a shared resource has to exit the critical section before another task can obtain access to the resource again. This ensures consistency of the shared resource and/or data.

The development of a comprehensive real-time scheduling theory, thus, has multiple objectives. First, it would permit one to rigorously specify a system. This leads to better *specifiability*, which, in turn, translates to ease of implementation later. Secondly, the timing behavior of the system becomes predictable and analyzable such that individual task timing requirements can be guaranteed, thereby lowering the costs of testing. Finally, the analyzable nature of the system readily supports incremental changes either to improve performance or to modify functionality, bypassing a costly new cycle of implementation, tuning and testing. It would set the stage for eliminating many of the timing dependent problems encountered in real-time systems today [Softech 86], thereby avoiding some of the most difficult problems to debug. This, in turn, results in an increase in system reliability, and reduced system integration time and cost. Because of the reduction in integration time, the ability to rapidly update system software will become possible and will result in improved operational readiness of the physical systems which the real-time computers control. In brief, a sound real-time scheduling theory would lead to better specifiability, predictability, analyzability, testability and maintainability of real-time systems. The net result would be a *science* of real-time systems.

1.2.1. Related Work

Real-time scheduling algorithms have been actively investigated, usually under idealized conditions [Lehoczky 86a, Leung 80, Liu 73, Zhao 87a]. The general real-time scheduling problem involves a set of real-time tasks and seeks to determine whether timing requirements of these tasks can be satisfied. Generally, there are two approaches that can be taken: the use of heuristics and the use of guaranteed schedulability analysis. The approach of using heuristics seeks near-optimal solutions. That is, this approach attempts to load the processor(s) to a very high degree of utilization and to meet the task deadlines most of the time. This approach often results in complex dynamic scheduling algorithms that can handle complex constraints. For example, Zhao, Stankovic and Ramamritham [Zhao 87b] investigated the use of heuristics to generate feasible schedules when tasks have resource constraints. Their heuristic has a high probability of generating a feasible schedule. The major tool for the study of heuristics is simulation, because heuristic algorithms are typically complex and are extremely difficult to analyze. This approach is particularly suited for highly dynamic real-time AI applications [Ramamritham 84, Stankovic 88].

The guaranteed schedulability analysis approach [Sha 87] is complementary to the approach of using heuristics and employs priority-driven preemptive scheduling techniques. A task or a task set is said to be *schedulable* if it meets all its deadlines. Hence, *schedulability* is the property of a task or a task set to be schedulable or not. Guaranteed schedulability analysis attempts to determine whether a task or task set will be schedulable under the worst-case conditions. It emphasizes the predictability of the timing behavior of the system. Both static priority and dynamic priority algorithms have been proposed. For example, Liu and Layland showed that the optimal static priority and dynamic priority scheduling algorithms for scheduling periodic tasks on a single processor are the rate-monotonic and the earliest deadline scheduling algorithms [Liu 73]. They proved that the processor utilizations below which any set of periodic tasks is guaranteed to be schedulable on a processor using the rate-monotonic and earliest deadline scheduling algorithms are $ln\,2$ (69%) and 100% respectively.

Mok [Mok 83] showed that the least slack-time algorithm is also an optimal algorithm for scheduling periodic tasks on a single processor, and also proved that the least slack-time algorithm dominates the earliest deadline scheduling algorithm in multiprocessor scheduling. Mok also considered the case when tasks use binary semaphores to enforce mutually exclusive access to shared resources, and proved that the determination of whether the tasks are schedulable is NP-hard. Leung and Merrill [Leung 80] showed that when the start time and the deadline for a task do not coincide with the period boundaries of a periodic task, determining whether a set of periodic tasks is schedulable using the earliest deadline scheduling algorithm is NP-hard. Leinbaugh [Leinbaugh 80] developed an algorithm that guarantees the response time of tasks with fixed resource constraints. Dhall and Liu [Dhall 78], and Lawler [Lawler 81] have considered rate-monotonic scheduling and deadline scheduling respectively on multiple processors.

1.3 SCOPE OF THIS BOOK

Much work on scheduling assumes that tasks executing on a real-time system are independent of one another and that they do not share any data and/or resources. However, tasks do share logical and physical resources and their accesses to these shared resources must be synchronized. Else, the consistency constraints of these shared resources can be compromised.

This book deals with scheduling concurrent tasks in a real-time system, where the tasks share resources and therefore must also synchronize with one another. Each task has its own resource requirements and its own timing constraints. We define and investigate real-time synchronization protocols for use on uniprocessors, multiprocessor systems and distributed real-time databases. We shall show that the properties of these protocols make it possible to predict and analyze the timing behavior of tasks using these protocols. As a result, the deadlines of real-time tasks can be guaranteed despite their synchronization requirements.

A basic goal of our synchronization protocols is to tightly bound the duration that a task would have to wait before obtaining access to a globally shared resource. Mok [Mok 83] showed that when tasks share data and use semaphores arbitrarily, then determining whether a given task set can meet its timing requirements is NP-hard even on a uniprocessor. However, our synchronization protocols would require new protocols to be used when semaphores are locked and released. By bounding the blocking durations of tasks, our synchronization protocols would allow us to derive sufficient conditions to test whether a given task set is schedulable. The protocols are designed such that task timing requirements will be satisfied at high levels of utilization and that an analysis of these protocols would be possible.

In brief, the goals of this book are two-fold:

- To develop synchronization protocols that will not only bound but minimize the amount of waiting time to access shared resources, and

- To analyze the behavior and performance of these protocols.

We shall formally prove the correctness of the protocols and their properties. We shall also derive sufficient conditions to test whether a set of tasks using the proposed protocol(s) will meet their deadlines. Performance studies of our protocols demonstrate that these protocols can not only provide better performance but also be implemented easily.

1.3.1. Approach Taken

We shall assume a priority-driven preemptive scheduling environment as the basis of our synchronization protocols. The protocols themselves would be defined independent of any scheduling algorithm. However, an analysis of these protocols will be based upon the rate-monotonic scheduling algorithm. The rate-monotonic scheduling algorithm assigns a fixed higher priority to a task with a shorter period and is guaranteed to schedule any set of n periodic tasks with a total processor utilization of less than $n(2^{1/n}-1)$. This utilization threshold converges to $ln\ 2$ (0.69) for large n. However, the average-case utilization threshold for the algorithm is 88% [Lehoczky 86b]. This means that high priority periodic tasks up to 69% utilization can be scheduled so that all task deadlines will always be met. If additional lower priority tasks are added, then on average an additional 19% utilization can be scheduled. With the period transformation method [Sha 86], we can ensure that the most important tasks fall into the 69% high priority group. This means that even if the processor experiences transient overloads, those tasks falling into the 69% group will still be guaranteed to meet their deadlines.

In addition to these results, many important practical problems that arise in the use of the rate-monotonic algorithm have been solved. They include the problem of integrated processor and I/O scheduling [Sha 86], the problem of insufficient priority levels and buffering when this algorithm is applied to a communication medium [Lehoczky 86a], and the problem of countering the effects of cycle-stealing [Rajkumar 87]. Recently, new algorithms have been developed to combine the scheduling of hard deadline periodic tasks and soft deadline aperiodic tasks [Lehoczky 87a, Sprunt 89, Strosnider 88]. These algorithms, called the *deferred server* and the *sporadic server* algorithms, have been shown to offer very large reductions in response times compared with traditional methods of scheduling in which aperiodic tasks are treated as background tasks or are serviced using polling techniques.

In contrast to the rate-monotonic scheduling algorithm, the earliest deadline scheduling algorithm can schedule any periodic task set up to a processor utilization of 100%. However, we base our work on the rate-monotonic scheduling algorithm for the following reasons. First, the rate-monotonic scheduling algorithm, on the average, can schedule a task set with a high processor utilization (88%), while the remaining (12%) utilization can still be used by aperiodic and background (maintenance) tasks. Secondly, if the earliest deadline scheduling algorithm is used, it is not possible to predict *a priori* which tasks will miss their deadlines under transient overloads. Finally, there does not seem to be tractable schemes under the deadline scheduling algorithm to solve the practical problems such as insufficient priority levels and buffering. In brief, the analysis of dynamic priority scheduling algorithms appears to be tractable only under idealized conditions and may not be so when certain practical constraints are added to the problem. On the other hand, static priority scheduling algorithms are analyzable for a wide range of problems, and the rate-monotonic algorithm is the optimal static priority scheduling algorithm with good performance, low complexity and minimal implementation overhead.

In summary, the rate-monotonic scheduling framework, within which our research fits well, appears to be a promising approach to the scientific design of real-time systems. The rate-monotonic scheduling framework allows the scheduling of periodic tasks on uniprocessors [Liu 73] and multiprocessors [Dhall 78], and can furthermore schedule aperiodic tasks with hard and soft deadlines [Sprunt 89, Strosnider 88], schedule messages on a bus with limited priority granularity [Lehoczky 86a], schedule LAN message traffic on token-rings [Strosnider 88], schedule DMA transactions [Rajkumar 87, Sprunt 88], include context-switching overhead, guarantee that critical deadlines will be met under transient overload conditions [Sha 86], accommodate deadlines prior to a period boundary and postponed deadlines at multiples of period boundaries, accomplish mode changes (faster than cyclical executives) [Sha 89], and support special caches that support predictable caching techniques [Kirk 88] etc. This book describes work that adds to this framework by permitting synchronization activities and resource-sharing among tasks. As a byproduct, the analysis of the protocols shall also allow non-instantaneous preemptions (as on bus transactions) to be accounted for in the framework.

1.4 ORGANIZATION OF THE BOOK

The rest of this book is organized as follows. In Chapter 2, we define the class of priority inheritance protocols that solve the uncontrolled priority inversion problem. Uncontrolled priority inversion is said to occur when a higher priority task is forced to wait for a lower priority task for an unbounded duration of time. We then analyze the properties of three important members of the family of priority inheritance protocols, namely the basic priority inheritance protocol, the priority ceiling protocol and the semaphore control protocol. The basic priority inheritance protocol avoids the uncontrolled priority inversion problem but still faces two problems: a task can be blocked for a long duration of time and mutual deadlocks can occur. Under the priority ceiling and semaphore control protocols, deadlocks are prevented and a task can be blocked for the duration of at most a single critical section. These properties not only make the timing behavior of tasks predictable but also lead to high schedulability. The priority ceiling protocol is unnecessarily restrictive in achieving its properties, and the semaphore control protocol removes these restrictions. These protocols are defined in terms of binary semaphores and can be used on uniprocessors. However, these protocols are also applicable to other synchronization primitives like monitors and the Ada rendezvous. We finally conduct experimental studies to compare the relative performance of the various uniprocessor synchronization protocols. The results clearly demonstrate the need for avoiding the unbounded priority problem.

Due to the additional concurrency inherent in multiple processor systems, the priority inversion problem becomes further compounded in the context of multiprocessors. In Chapter 3, we study the priority inversion problem in a system with more than one processor, and show that the concept of priority inversion needs to be extended to include remote blocking. In specific, we develop two synchronization protocols, one for use in shared memory multiprocessors and another for use in distributed systems. As may be expected, the parallel nature of the underlying configuration conflicts with the serialization constraints of synchronization resulting in much longer blocking durations.

In Chapter 4, we develop synchronization protocols for use in distributed real-time databases. In database transactions, locks on objects need not be exclusive but can be based on the nature of the transaction being carried out on a database object. We investigate the semantics of read-write locks in the context of real-time databases, and show that compatible locks are not necessarily useful in this context. We extend the priority ceiling protocol to exploit lock compatibility only when it leads to a better guaranteed performance. Finally, we discuss the application of this protocol to a distributed real-time database.

Finally, in Chapter 5, we summarize the primary results of this book, and discuss future directions in which this work needs to be extended.

A glossary of symbols used throughout the book is given in Appendix B for
quick reference.

Chapter Two

Real-Time Synchronization in Uniprocessors

2.1 INTRODUCTION

Priority-driven preemptive scheduling is an approach used in many real-time systems. The importance of this approach is underscored by the fact that Ada, the language mandated by the US Department of Defense for all its real-time systems, supports such a scheduling discipline [Ada 83]. Much of the scheduling work typically assumes perfect preemption, the assumption that a higher priority task can preempt a lower priority task being run with no penalties in time. An important problem that has not been extensively studied in the real-time scheduling literature is the problem of blocking caused by the synchronization of tasks that share physical or logical resources.

Unfortunately, task blocking is a common occurrence and must be considered. Blocking occurs when a request is made for a resource which has mutual exclusion requirements and is already in use. The most common situation occurs when two tasks attempt to access shared data. To maintain consistency, the access must be serialized. If the higher priority task gains access first, then the proper priority order is maintained. However, if the higher priority task arrives after the lower priority task gains access to the shared data, then priority inversion takes place. *Priority inversion* is said to occur when a higher priority task must wait for the processing of a lower priority task. If priority inversion is not controlled, it becomes impossible to determine whether tasks can meet their deadlines. However, a direct application of the synchronization mechanisms like the Ada rendezvous, semaphores or monitors can lead to uncontrolled priority inversion, a high priority task being blocked by a lower priority job for an indefinite period of time.

Prolonged durations of priority inversion can lead to the missing of deadlines even at a low level of processor utilization. The level of processor utilization attainable before deadlines are missed is referred to as the *schedulability* of the system. To maintain a high degree of schedulability, protocols that would minimize the amount of blocking are essential. It is also important to be able to analyze the performance of any proposed protocol in order to determine the schedulability of real-time tasks that use this protocol.

In particular, we shall formally investigate the *priority inheritance protocols* as a priority management scheme for synchronization primitives that remedies the uncontrolled priority inversion problem. We shall formally define the protocols in terms of binary semaphores, but the protocols are equally applicable to other synchronization primitives such as monitors and the Ada rendezvous. In this chapter, we shall focus only upon the uniprocessor environment.

2.2 PRIORITY INHERITANCE PROTOCOLS

Common synchronization primitives include semaphores, locks, monitors and the Ada rendezvous. Although the use of these or equivalent methods is necessary to protect the consistency of shared data and hence the correctness of computations, their use may jeopardize the ability of the system to satisfy task timing requirements. In fact, all of these commonly used synchronization mechanisms can lead to an indefinite duration of priority inversion. A simple example of the problems that can arise is the following and was perhaps first described by Lampson and Redell [Lampson 80]. In the following, a *job* is considered to be one instance of a task.

> **Example 2.1:** Let J_1, J_2 and J_3 be three jobs arranged in descending order of priority. Let jobs J_1 and J_3 share a common data structure guarded by a binary semaphore S. Suppose that J_3 locks the semaphore S and enters its critical section at time t_0. While J_3 is still within its critical section, J_1 arrives and having a higher priority preempts J_3. Later J_1 attempts to lock S and is blocked. One might expect that J_1, being the highest priority job, will be blocked for no longer than the duration for J_3 to exit its critical section. However, the duration of J_1's blocking

is, in fact, unpredictable. This is because J_3 can be preempted by the intermediate priority job J_2. The blocking of J_3, and hence that of J_1, will continue until J_2 and other pending intermediate priority jobs are completed.

The duration of priority inversion for Job J_1 in Example 2.1 can be arbitrarily long. The delay worsens when the intermediate priority jobs are instances of periodic tasks. This situation can be partially remedied if a job in its critical section is not allowed to be preempted; however, this solution is only appropriate for very short critical sections, because it creates unnecessary blocking. For instance, once a low priority job enters a long critical section, a high priority job which does not access the shared data structure may be needlessly blocked. An identical problem exists in the use of monitors. In the case of the Ada rendezvous, when a high priority job (task) is waiting in the entry queue of a server job, the server itself can be preempted by an independent job J, if job J's priority is higher than both the priority of the server and the job which is currently in rendezvous with the server. Raising the server priority to the highest level would avoid this particular problem but would create a new problem: a low priority job can now block the execution of independent higher priority jobs via the use of the server.

The use of *priority inheritance protocols* is one approach to rectify the priority inversion problem inherent in existing synchronization primitives. Before we present these protocols, we first define the basic concepts and state our assumptions. A *job* is a sequence of instructions that will continuously use the processor until its completion if it is executing alone on the processor. We assume that jobs do not suspend themselves, say for I/O operations; however, such a situation can be accommodated by defining two or more jobs. In all our discussions below, we assume that jobs J_1, J_2, $\cdots$, J_n are listed in descending order of priority with J_1 having the highest priority. A *periodic task* is a sequence of the same type of job occurring at regular intervals, and an *aperiodic task* is a sequence of the same type of job occurring at irregular intervals. Each task is assigned a fixed priority, and every job of the same task is assigned that task's priority. If two jobs are eligible to run, the higher priority job will be run. Jobs with the same priority are executed in a FCFS discipline. We assume that each instance of a periodic task must be completed by the time its next instance arrives.

We now state the notation used to represent critical sections and job priorities.

Notation:

- A binary semaphore guarding a shared data or resource is denoted by S_i.

- $z_{i,j,k}$ represents the kth critical section in job J_i guarded by S_j. This notation is necessary because job J_i may access the semaphore S_j more than once. $z_{i,j}$ denotes an arbitrary member of the set $\{z_{i,j,k}, k \geq 1\}$. This notation is shortened to z_i, if the corresponding semaphore S_j is not of interest.

- $p(J_i)$ denotes the priority of job J_i.

- $P(S_i)$ and $V(S_i)$ denote the indivisible operations *wait* and *signal* respectively on the binary semaphore S_i.

We assume that each shared data structure is guarded by a binary semaphore and define the protocols that we propose in terms of binary semaphores. However, the idea is also applicable when monitors or rendezvous are used. We also assume that a job will not attempt to lock a semaphore it has already locked and thus deadlock with itself[1]. In addition, we assume that locks on semaphores will be released before or at the end of a job.

A job can have multiple non-overlapping critical sections, e.g.

$$\{ \cdots P(S_1) \cdots V(S_1) \cdots P(S_2) \cdots V(S_2) \cdots \}$$

or nested critical sections, e.g.

$$\{ \cdots P(S_1) \cdots P(S_2) \cdots V(S_2) \cdots V(S_1) \cdots \}.$$

In the latter case, the outer critical section $z_{i,1}$ bounded by $P(S_1)$ and

---

[1] It is, nevertheless, possible to detect and abort such self-deadlocks during run-time.

$V(S_1)$ contains the inner critical section $z_{i,2}$ bounded by $P(S_2)$ and $V(S_2)$[2]. The term "critical section" will be used to denote any critical section between a $P(S)$ and the corresponding $V(S)$. This term includes both the outermost part of a nested critical section and also the inner part(s) of a nested critical section. The "duration of execution of a critical section" is defined to be the time to execute the code between the (outermost) P and its corresponding V operations when the job executes alone on the processor.

In the next two sections, we will introduce the concept of priority inheritance and define three priority inheritance protocols. An important feature of these protocols is that one can develop a schedulability analysis for them in the sense that a schedulability bound can be determined. If the utilization of the task set stays below this bound, then the deadlines of all the tasks can be guaranteed. In order to create such a bound, it is necessary to determine the worst-case duration of priority inversion that any task can encounter. This worst-case blocking duration will depend upon the particular protocol in use but the following approach will always be taken.

<u>Notation</u>: Let $\beta_{i,j} = \{z_{j,k} \mid j>i$ and $z_{j,k}$ can block $J_i\}$ be the set of all critical sections of the lower priority job J_j which can block J_i.

Since we consider only properly nested critical sections, the set of blocking critical sections is partially ordered by set inclusion. Using this partial ordering, we can reduce our attention to the set of maximal elements of $\beta_{i,j}$, $\beta_{i,j}^*$. Specifically, we have

$$\beta_{i,j}^* = \{z_{j,k} \mid z_{j,k} \in \beta_{i,j} \text{ and } \sim\exists \beta \in \beta_{i,j} \text{ such that } z_{i,j} \subset \beta\}.$$

The set $\beta_{i,j}^*$ contains the longest critical sections of J_j which can block J_i and eliminates redundant inner critical sections. For purposes of schedulability analysis, we will restrict attention to $\beta^* = \cup_{j>i} \beta_{i,j}^*$, the set of all longest critical sections that can block J_i.

---

[2]For the sake of simplicity, we do not explicitly consider an "overlapped" critical section such as $\{P(S_1) \cdots P(S_2) \cdots V(S_1) \cdots V(S_2)\}$. The properties of the protocols presented in this book would be similar in the presence of overlapped critical sections, but will not be dealt with explicitly for the sake of simplicity.

Finally, we assume a uniprocessor which is executing a fixed set of known tasks.

2.3 THE BASIC PRIORITY INHERITANCE PROTOCOL

The basic idea of priority inheritance protocols is that when a job J blocks higher priority jobs, it executes its critical section at the highest priority level of all of the blocked jobs. After exiting its critical section, job J returns to its original priority level. To illustrate this idea, we apply this protocol to Example 2.1. Suppose that job J_1 is blocked by job J_3. The priority inheritance protocol stipulates that job J_3 execute its critical section at job J_1's priority. As a result, job J_2 will be unable to preempt job J_3 and will itself be blocked. That is, the higher priority job J_2 must wait for the critical section of the lower priority job J_3 to be executed, because job J_3 "inherits" the priority of job J_1. Otherwise, J_1 will be indirectly preempted by J_2. When J_3 exits its critical section, it regains its assigned lowest priority and awakens J_1 which was blocked by J_3. Job J_1, having the highest priority, immediately preempts J_3 and runs to completion. This enables J_2 and J_3 to resume in succession and run to completion. On the other hand, suppose that job J_2, instead of J_1, shares the semaphore with J_3 and is blocked by job J_3. In this case, job J_3 executes its critical section at the priority of J_2. If job J_1 is ready to execute, it will preempt job J_3 and hence J_2. This is appropriate, since both job J_2 and J_3 should be preempted by job J_1.

Definition: A real-time synchronization protocol Θ is said to be a priority inheritance protocol, if under Θ a low priority job J blocks higher priority jobs J_1, J_2, $\cdots$, J_k, J will execute at a priority of $max(\mathsf{p}(J_1), \mathsf{p}(J_2), \cdots, \mathsf{p}(J_k))$.

A whole class of priority inheritance protocols can be defined by granting a semaphore to a job J only under certain conditions. If the semaphore is not granted, job J blocks, and the job(s) that can unblock J inherit J's priority. Under the basic inheritance protocol, a job J requesting a semaphore S blocks only if S has already been granted to a different job.

2.3.1. The Definition of The Basic Protocol

We now define the basic priority inheritance protocol.

1. Job J, which has the highest priority among the jobs ready to run, is assigned the processor. Before job J enters a critical section, it must first obtain the lock on the semaphore S guarding the critical section. Job J will be blocked and the lock on S will be denied, if semaphore S has been already locked. In this case, job J is said to be blocked by the job which holds the lock on S. Otherwise, job J will obtain the lock on semaphore S and enter its critical section. When a job J exits its critical section, the binary semaphore associated with the critical section will be unlocked and the highest priority job, if any, blocked by job J will be awakened.

2. A job J uses its assigned priority, unless it is in its critical section and blocks higher priority jobs. If job J blocks higher priority jobs, J *inherits* $p(J_H)$, the highest priority of the jobs blocked by J. When J exits a critical section, it resumes the priority it had at the point of entry into the critical section[3].

3. Priority inheritance is transitive. For instance, suppose J_1, J_2 and J_3 are three jobs in descending order of priority. Then, if job J_3 blocks job J_2, and J_2 blocks job J_1, J_3 would inherit the priority of J_1 via J_2. Finally, the operations of priority inheritance and of the resumption of original priority must be indivisible.

4. A job J can preempt another job J_L if job J is not blocked and its priority is higher than the priority, inherited or assigned, at which job J_L is executing.

It is helpful to summarize that under the basic priority inheritance protocol, a high priority job can be blocked by a low priority job in one of two situations. First, there is the *direct* blocking, a situation in which a higher priority job attempts to lock a locked semaphore. Direct blocking is necessary to ensure the consistency of shared data. Second, a medium

---

[3]Thus, when J executes $V(S_2)$ in $\{P(S_1) \cdots P(S_2), \cdots, V(S_2), \cdots, V(S_1)\}$, it reverts to the priority it had before it executed $P(S_2)$. This may be lower than its current executing priority and cause J to be preempted by a higher priority task. J would, of course, still hold the lock on S_1.

priority job J_1 can be blocked by a low priority job J_2, which inherits the priority of a high priority job J_0. We refer to this form of blocking as *push-through* blocking, which is necessary to avoid having a high priority job J_0 being indirectly preempted by the execution of a medium priority job J_1.

2.3.2. Implementing the Basic Priority Inheritance Protocol

The implementation of the basic priority inheritance protocol is rather straightforward. It requires a priority queueing of jobs blocked on a semaphore and indivisible system calls *Lock_Semaphore* and *Release_Semaphore*. These system calls perform the priority inheritance operation, in addition to the traditional operations of locking, unlocking and semaphore queue maintenance.

2.3.3. Properties of the Basic Priority Inheritance Protocol

We now proceed to analyze the properties of the basic priority inheritance protocol defined above. In this section, we assume that deadlock is prevented by some external means, e.g., semaphores are accessed in an order that is consistent with a pre-defined acyclical order. Throughout this section, β_i and β_i^* refer to the sets of critical sections that can block J_i when the basic priority inheritance protocol is used.

> **Lemma 2-1:** A job J_H can be blocked by a lower priority job J_L, only if J_L is executing within a critical section $z_{H,L} \in \beta_{H,L}^*$, when J is initiated.
>
> **Proof:** By the definitions of the basic priority inheritance protocol and the blocking set $\beta_{H,L}^*$, task J_L can block J_H only if it directly blocks J_H or has its priority raised above J_H through priority inheritance. In either case, the critical section $z_{H,L}$ currently being executed by J_L is in $\beta_{H,L}^*$. If J_L is not within a critical section which cannot directly block J_H and cannot lead to the inheritance of a priority higher than J_H, then J_L can be preempted by J_H and can never block it.

> **Lemma 2-2:** Under the basic priority inheritance protocol, a high priority job J_H can be blocked by a lower priority job J_L for at most the duration of one critical section of $\beta_{H,L}^*$ regardless of the number of semaphores J_H and J_L share.

Proof: By Lemma 2-1, for J_L to block J_H, J_L must be currently executing a critical section $z_{H,L} \in \beta_{H,L}^*$. Once J_L exits $z_{H,L}$, it can be preempted by J_H and J_H cannot be blocked by J_L again.

Theorem 2-3: Under the basic priority inheritance protocol, given a job J_0 for which there are n lower priority jobs $\{J_1, \ldots, J_n\}$, job J_0 can be blocked for at most the duration of one critical section in *each* of $\beta_{0,i}^*$, $1 \le i \le n$.

Proof: By Lemma 2-2, each of the n lower priority jobs can block job J_0 for at most the duration of a single critical section in each of the blocking sets $\beta_{0,i}^*$.

We now determine the bound on the blockings as a function of the semaphores shared by jobs.

Lemma 2-4: A semaphore S can cause push-through blocking to job J, only if S is accessed both by a job which has priority lower than that of J and by a job which has priority equal to or higher than that of J.

Proof: Suppose that J_L accesses semaphore S and has priority lower than that of J. According to the priority inheritance protocol, if S is not accessed by a job with priority equal to or higher than that of J, then job J_L's critical section guarded by S cannot inherit a priority equal to or higher than that of J. In this case, job J_L will be preempted by job J and the Lemma follows.

We next define

$$\beta_{i,j,k}^* = \{z_{i,j} | z_{i,j} \in \beta_{i,j}^* \text{ and } s_{i,j} = S_k\},$$

the set of all longest critical sections of job J_j which correspond to locking semaphore S_k and can block job J_i either directly or via push-through blocking.

Let $\beta_{i,.,k}^* = \cup_{j \ge i} \beta_{i,j,k}^*$ represent the set of all longest critical sections corresponding to semaphore S_k which can block J_i.

Lemma 2-5: Under the basic priority inheritance protocol, a job

J_i can encounter blocking by at most one critical section of $\beta^*_{i,.,k}$ for each semaphore S_k, $1 \le k \le m$, where m is the number of distinct semaphores.

Proof: By Lemma 2-1, job J_L can block a higher priority job J_H if J_L is currently executing a critical section in $\beta^*_{H,L}$. Any such critical section corresponds to the locking and unlocking of a semaphore S_k. Since we deal only with binary semaphores, only one of the lower priority jobs can be within a blocking critical section corresponding to a particular semaphore S_k. Once this critical section is exited, the lower priority job J_L can no longer block J_H. Consequently, only one critical section in β^*_i corresponding to semaphore S_k can block J_H. The Lemma follows.

Theorem 2-6: Under the basic priority inheritance protocol, if there are m semaphores which can block job J, then J can be blocked by at most m times.

Proof: It follows from Lemma 2-5 that job J can be blocked at most once by each of the m semaphores.

Theorems 2-3 and 2-6 place an upper bound on the *total* blocking delay that a job can encounter. Given these results, it is possible to determine at compile-time the worst-case blocking duration of a job (assuming that deadlock is prevented by some technique such as the partial ordering of resource accesses). For instance, if there are four semaphores which can potentially block job J and there are three other lower priority tasks, J may be blocked for a maximum duration of three longest critical sections. Moreover, one can find the worst-case blocking duration for a job by studying the durations of the critical sections in $\beta^*_{i,j}$ and $\beta^*_{i,.,k}$. A branch-and-bound scheme to determine the worst-case blocking duration of a task is described in Appendix A.

Still, the basic priority inheritance protocol has the following two problems. First, this basic protocol, by itself, does not prevent deadlocks. For example, suppose that at time t_1, job J_2 locks semaphore S_2 and enters its critical section. At time t_2, job J_2 attempts to make a nested access to lock semaphore S_1. However, job J_1, a higher priority job, is ready at this time. Job J_1 preempts job J_2 and locks semaphore S_1. Next, if job J_1 tries to lock semaphore S_2, a deadlock is formed.

The deadlock problem can be solved, say, by imposing a total ordering on the semaphore accesses. Still, a second problem exists. The blocking duration for a job, though bounded, can still be substantial, because a task may be blocked for the duration of multiple critical sections. For instance, suppose that J_1 needs to sequentially access S_1 and S_2. Also suppose that J_2 preempts J_3 within the critical section $z_{3,1}$ and enters the critical section $z_{2,2}$. Job J_1 is initiated at this instant and finds that the semaphores S_1 and S_2 have been respectively locked by the lower priority jobs J_3 and J_2. As a result, J_1 would be blocked for the duration of two critical sections, once to wait for J_3 to release S_1 and again to wait for J_2 to release S_2. Thus, multiple blockings can occur.

Our next goal is to develop a priority inheritance protocol that avoids both multiple blocking and deadlocks resulting from the basic priority inheritance protocol. Intuitively, it can be seen that the basic priority inheritance protocol runs into its problems for the following reason. An unlocked semaphore is allowed to be locked at any instant irrespective of its relationship to the semaphores that have been already locked. Hence, when a higher priority job arrives, it can find that several semaphores that it needs have been locked by lower priority jobs. Furthermore, such uncontrolled locking can potentially cause a deadlock as well. This situation can be remedied by allowing semaphores to be locked only under selective conditions. In other words, if the locking of a semaphore may cause multiple blockings to a higher priority job, a lock on the semaphore will not be granted. We use the information about the semaphore needs of each job and the job priorities to decide whether the locking of a semaphore can lead to multiple blocking and/or deadlock.

2.4 THE PRIORITY CEILING PROTOCOL

2.4.1. Overview

The goal of this protocol is to prevent the formation of deadlocks and of multiple blocking. The underlying idea of this protocol is to ensure that when a job J preempts the critical section of another job and executes its own critical section z, the priority at which this new critical section z will execute is guaranteed to be higher than the (inherited) priorities of all the preempted critical sections. If this condition cannot be satisfied, job J is denied entry into the critical section z and suspended, and the job that blocks J inherits J's priority. This idea is realized by first assigning a priority ceiling to each semaphore, which is equal to the highest priority task that may use this semaphore. We then allow a job J to start a new critical section only if J's priority is higher than all priority ceilings of all the semaphores locked by jobs other than J. Example 2.2 illustrates this idea and the deadlock avoidance property while Example 2.3 illustrates the avoidance of multiple blocking.

The priority ceiling protocol (PCP) will be shown to be actually an approximation of the semaphore control protocol (SCP) that we shall develop in Section 2.5. However, PCP is of special significance due to its very low complexity and subsequent ease of implementation. Readers not interested in relatively complex mechanisms to synchronize real-time tasks may, therefore, skip the discussion on SCP, and read those pertaining to PCP only.

Definition: The *priority ceiling* of a semaphore is defined as the priority of the highest priority job that may lock this semaphore. The priority ceiling of a semaphore S, denoted by $c(S_j)$, represents the highest priority that a critical section guarded by S can inherit from a higher priority job. In other words, if a job J locks the semaphore S, the corresponding critical section of J can inherit at most a priority equal to the priority ceiling of S.

Example 2.2: Suppose that we have three jobs J_0, J_1 and J_2 in the system. In addition, there are two shared data structures protected by the binary semaphores S_1 and S_2 respectively. Suppose the sequence of processing steps for each job is as follows.

$$J_0 = \{ \cdots, \mathbf{P}(S_0), \cdots, \mathbf{V}(S_0), \cdots \}$$

$$J_1 = \{ \cdots, \mathbf{P}(S_1), \cdots, \mathbf{P}(S_2), \cdots, \mathbf{V}(S_2), \cdots, \mathbf{V}(S_1), \cdots \}$$

$$J_2 = \{ \cdots, \mathbf{P}(S_2), \cdots, \mathbf{P}(S_1), \cdots, \mathbf{V}(S_1), \cdots, \mathbf{V}(S_2), \cdots \}$$

Recall that the priority of job J_1 is assumed to be higher than that of job J_2. Thus, the priority ceilings of both semaphores S_1 and S_2 are equal to the priority of job J_1.

The sequence of events described below is depicted in Figure 2-1.

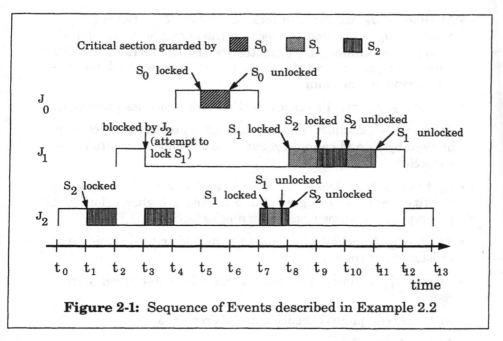

Figure 2-1: Sequence of Events described in Example 2.2

A line at a low level indicates that the corresponding job is blocked or has been preempted by a higher priority job. A line raised to a higher level indicates that the job is executing. The absence of a line indicates that the job has not yet been initiated or has completed. Shaded portions indicate execution of critical sections. Suppose that

- At time t_0, J_2 is initiated and begins execution.
- At time t_1, J_2 locks semaphore S_2.
- At time t_2, job J_1 is initiated and preempts job J_2.
- At time t_3, job J_1 tries to enter its critical section by making an indivisible system call to execute $\mathbf{P}(S_1)$. However, the run-time system finds that S_2 is locked, and $\mathsf{p}(J_1) < \mathsf{c}(S_2)$. Hence, the run-time system suspends job J_1 without locking S_1. Job J_2 now *inherits* the priority of job J_1 and resumes execution. Note that J_1 is blocked outside its critical section. As J_1 is not given the lock on S_1 but suspended instead, the potential deadlock involving J_1 and J_2 is prevented.
- At time t_4, J_2 is still in its critical section and the highest priority job J_0 is initiated and preempts J_2.

- At time t_5, J_0 attempts to lock semaphore S_0. Since $p(J_0) > c(S_2)$, job J_0 is granted the lock on the semaphore S_0. Job J_0 therefore continues and executes its critical section, thereby effectively preempting J_2 in its critical section and not encountering any blocking.

- At time t_6, J_0 exits its critical section and continues execution.

- At time t_7, J_0 completes execution. Job J_2 resumes, since J_1 is blocked by J_2 and cannot execute. J_2 continues execution and locks S_1.

- By time t_8, J_2 releases S_1 and S_2 and resumes its assigned priority. Now, J_1 is signaled and having a higher priority, it preempts J_2, resumes execution and locks S_1.

- At time t_9, J_1 locks S_2, executes the nested critical section and unlocks S_2 at time t_{10}.

- At time t_{11}, it unlocks S_1 and executes its non-critical section code.

- At t_{12}, J_1 completes execution and J_2 resumes.

- At t_{13}, J_2 completes.

Note that in the above example, J_0 is never blocked because its priority is higher than the priority ceilings of semaphores S_1 and S_2. J_1 was blocked by the lower priority job J_2 during the intervals $[t_3, t_4]$ and $[t_7, t_8]$. However, these intervals correspond to part of the duration that J_2 needs to lock S_2. Thus, J_1 is blocked for no more than the duration of one critical section of a lower priority job J_2 even though the actual blocking occurs over disjoint time intervals. It is, indeed, a property of this protocol that any job can be blocked for at most the duration of a single critical section of a lower priority job. This property is further illustrated by the following example.

Example 2.3: Consider the example from the previous section where the highest priority task encounters multiple blockings. We assumed that job J_1 needs to access S_1 and S_2 sequentially while J_2 accesses S_2 and J_3 accesses S_1. Hence, $c(S_1) = c(S_2) = p(J_1)$. As before, let job J_3 lock S_1 at time t_0. At time t_1, job J_2 is initiated and preempts J_3. However, at time t_2, when J_2 attempts to lock S_2, the run-time system finds that S_1 is locked, and $p(J_2) < c(S_1) = p(J_1)$. Hence, J_2 is denied the lock on S_2 and blocked. Job J_3 resumes execution at J_2's priority. At time t_3, when J_3 is still in its critical section, J_1 is initiated and finds that only one semaphore S_1 is locked. At time t_4, J_1 is blocked by J_3 which holds the lock on S_1. Hence, J_3 inherits the priority of J_1. At time t_5, job J_3 exits its critical section $z_{3,1}$, resumes its original priority and awakens J_1. Job J_1, having the highest priority, preempts J_3 and runs to completion. Next, J_2 which is no longer blocked completes its execution and is followed by J_3.

Again, note that J_1 is blocked by J_3 within the interval $[t_4, t_5]$ which corresponds to the single critical section $z_{3,1}$. Also, job J_2 is blocked by J_3 between the disjoint intervals $[t_2, t_3]$ and $[t_4, t_5]$ which also correspond to the same critical section $z_{3,1}$.

2.4.2. Definition of the Priority Ceiling Protocol

Having illustrated the basic idea of PCP and its properties, we now present its definition .

Job J, which has the highest priority among the jobs ready to run, is assigned the processor, and let S^* be the semaphore with the highest priority ceiling of all semaphores currently locked by jobs other than job J.

1. Before job J enters a critical section, it must first obtain the lock on the semaphore S guarding the shared data structure. Job J will be blocked and the lock on S will be denied, if the priority of job J is not higher than the priority ceiling of semaphore S^*.[4] In this case, job J is said to be blocked on semaphore S^* and to be blocked by the job which holds the lock on S^*. Otherwise, job J will obtain the lock on semaphore S and enter its critical section. When a job J exits its critical section, the binary semaphore associated with the critical section will be unlocked and the highest priority job, if any, blocked by job J will be awakened.

---

[4]Note that if S has been already locked, the priority ceiling of S will be at least equal to the priority of J. Because job J's priority is not higher than the priority ceiling of the semaphore S locked by another job, J will be blocked. Hence, this rule implies that if a job J attempts to lock a semaphore that has been already locked, J will be denied the lock and blocked instead.

2. A job J uses its assigned priority, unless it is in its critical section and blocks higher priority jobs. If job J blocks higher priority jobs, J *inherits* $p(J_H)$, the highest priority of the jobs blocked by J. When J exits a critical section, it resumes the priority it had at the point of entry into the critical section. Priority inheritance is transitive. Finally, the operations of priority inheritance and of the resumption of previous priority must be indivisible.

3. A job J, when it does not attempt to enter a critical section, can preempt another job J_L if its priority is higher than the priority, inherited or assigned, at which job J_L is executing.

We shall illustrate PCP using an example.

Example 2.4: We assume that the priority of job J_i is higher than that of job J_{i+1}. The processing steps in each job are as follows:

Job J_0 accesses $z_{0,0}$ and $z_{0,1}$ by executing the steps

$$\{\cdots, \mathbf{P}(S_0), \cdots, \mathbf{V}(S_0), \cdots, \mathbf{P}(S_1), \cdots, \mathbf{V}(S_1), \cdots\},$$

job J_1 accesses only $z_{1,2}$ by executing

$$\{\cdots, \mathbf{P}(S_2), \cdots, \mathbf{V}(S_2), \cdots\},$$

and job J_2 accesses $z_{2,2}$ and makes a nested semaphore access to S_1 by executing

$$\{\cdots, \mathbf{P}(S_2), \cdots, \mathbf{P}(S_1), \cdots, \mathbf{V}(S_1), \cdots, \mathbf{V}(S_2), \cdots\}.$$

Note that $c(S_0) = c(S_1) = p(J_0)$, and $c(S_2) = p(J_1)$. Figure 2-2 depicts the sequence of events described below.

Suppose that

• At time t_0, job J_2 begins execution.

• At time t_1, J_2 locks S_2.

• At time t_2, job J_1 is initiated, preempts J_2 and begins execution.

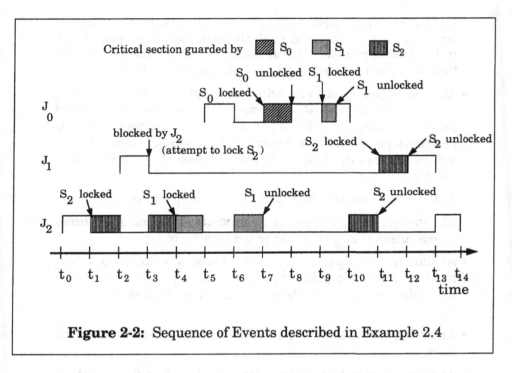

Figure 2-2: Sequence of Events described in Example 2.4

- At time t_3, while attempting to access S_2 already locked by J_2, job J_1 becomes blocked. Job J_2 now resumes the execution of its critical section $z_{2,2}$ at its inherited priority of J_1, namely $p(J_1)$.

- At time t_4, job J_2 successfully enters its nested critical section $z_{2,1}$ by locking S_1. Job J_2 is allowed to lock S_1, because there is no semaphore S^* which is locked by other jobs and which has priority ceiling higher than the priority of J_2. Job J_2 executes $z_{2,1}$ at priority $p(J_1)$, because this is the priority of the highest priority job currently blocked by J_2.

- At time t_5, job J_2 is still executing $z_{2,1}$ but the highest priority job J_0 is initiated. Job J_0 preempts J_2 within $z_{2,1}$ and executes its own non-critical section code. This is possible because $p(J_0) > p(J_1)$, the inherited priority level at which job J_2's $z_{2,1}$ was being executed.

- At time t_6, job J_0 attempts to enter its critical section $z_{0,0}$ by locking S_0, which is not locked by any job. However, since $p(J_0) = c(S_1)$, the protocol condition fails. That is, job J_0 is blocked by job J_2 which holds the lock on S_1. This is a new form of blocking introduced by the priority ceiling protocol in addition to the direct and push-through blocking encountered in the basic protocol. At this point, job J_2 resumes its execution of $z_{2,1}$ at the newly inherited priority level of $p(J_0)$.

- At time t_7, job J_2 exits its critical section $z_{2,1}$. Semaphore S_1 is now unlocked, job J_2 returns to the previously inherited priority of $p(J_1)$, and job J_0 is awakened. At this point, J_0 preempts job J_2, and its priority $p(J_0) > c(S_2)$. Hence, job J_0 will be granted the lock on S_0 and will execute its critical section $z_{0,0}$.

- At time t_8, J_0 unlocks S_0, locks S_1 at time t_9 and unlocks S_1.

- At time t_{10}, job J_0 completes its execution, and job J_2 resumes its execution of $z_{2,2}$ at its inherited priority $p(J_1)$.

- At time t_{11}, job J_2 exits $z_{2,2}$, semaphore S_2 is unlocked, job J_2 returns to its own priority $p(J_2)$ and job J_1 is awakened. At this point, job J_1 preempts job J_2 and J_1 is granted the lock on S_2.

- At time t_{12}, J_1 unlocks S_2 and executes its non-critical section code.

- At time t_{13}, job J_1 completes its execution and finally job J_2 resumes its execution, until it also completes at time t_{14}.

PCP introduces a third type of blocking in addition to direct blocking and push-through blocking caused by the basic priority inheritance protocol. An instance of this new type of blocking occurs at time t_6 in the above example. We shall refer to this form of blocking as *ceiling blocking*. Ceiling blocking is needed for the avoidance of deadlock and of multiple blocking. This avoidance approach belongs to the class of pessimistic protocols which sometimes create unnecessary blocking. Although the PCP introduces a new form of blocking, the worst-case blocking is dramatically improved. Under the basic priority inheritance protocol, a job J can be blocked for at most the duration of $min(n, m)$ critical sections, where n is the number of lower priority jobs that could block J and m is the number of semaphores that can be used to block J. On the contrary, under PCP, a job J can be blocked for at most the duration of one longest critical section of a lower priority task.

2.4.3. An Implementation of the Priority Ceiling Protocol

The implementation of the priority ceiling protocol entails more changes than the basic inheritance protocol. The most notable change is that we no longer maintain semaphore queues. The traditional ready queue is replaced by a single job queue *Job_Q*. The job queue is a priority-ordered list of jobs ready to run or blocked by the ceiling protocol. The job at the head of the queue is assumed to be currently running. We need only a single prioritized job queue because under the priority ceiling protocol, the job with the highest (inherited) priority is always eligible to execute. Finally, the run-time system also maintains *S_List*, a list of currently locked semaphores ordered according to their priority ceilings. Each semaphore *S* stores the information of the job, if any, that holds the lock on *S* and the ceiling of *S*. Indivisible system calls *Lock_Semaphore* and *Release_Semaphore* maintain *Job_Q* and *S_List*. An example implementation of this scheme on an Ada run-time system can be seen in [Borger 89]. The function *Lock_Semaphore* could also easily detect a self-deadlock where a job blocks on itself. Since the run-time system associates with each semaphore the job that holds the lock on it, a direct comparison of a job requesting a lock and the job that holds the lock determines whether a self-deadlock has occurred. If such a self-deadlock does occur, typically due to programmer error, the job could be aborted and an error message delivered.

The priority ceiling protocol exhibits some special properties that can be potentially exploited to provide a streamlined implementation. We shall list these properties and shall omit proving these properties due to their simplicity. Under this protocol, a job can be blocked *only* on the first semaphore that it requests. That is, once it obtains this semaphore, it will always be granted all subsequent semaphore requests until it completes or suspends itself. Again, since the lowest priority task cannot encounter any blocking, it will never be blocked on any semaphore request. A push-down stack of locked semaphores *S_Stack* can be maintained instead of traditional semaphore queues. This semaphore stack automatically orders semaphores according to their priority ceilings. When a semaphore *S* is locked, it is pushed onto the *S_Stack* if its priority ceiling is higher than the priority ceiling of the semaphore at the head of *S_Stack*. Whenever a context switch occurs, a pointer is updated to point to the last semaphore pushed by the preempted task.

2.4.4. The Properties of The Priority Ceiling Protocol

Before we prove the properties of this protocol, it is important to recall the two basic assumptions about jobs. First, a job is assumed to be a sequence of instructions that will continuously execute until its completion, when it executes alone on a processor. Second, a job will release all of its locks, if it ever holds any, before or at the end of its execution. The relaxation of our first assumption is addressed at the end of this section. Throughout this section, the sets $\beta_{i,j}$, $\beta_{i,j}^*$ and β_i^* refer to the blocking sets associated with PCP.

<u>Remark</u>: Lemma 2-1 is true under PCP.

Lemma 2-7: A job J can be blocked by a lower priority job J_L, only if the priority of job J is no higher than the highest priority ceiling of all the semaphores that are locked by job J_L when J is initiated.

Proof: Suppose that when J is initiated, the priority of job J is higher than the highest priority ceiling of all the semaphores that are currently locked by job J_L. By the definition of PCP, job J can always preempt the execution of job J_L, and the Lemma follows.

Lemma 2-8: Suppose that the critical section $z_{j,n}$ of job J_j is preempted by job J_i which enters its critical section $z_{i,m}$. Under PCP, job J_j cannot inherit a priority level which is higher than or equal to that of job J_i until job J_i completes.

Proof: Suppose that job J_j inherits a priority that is higher than or equal to that of job J_i before J_i completes. Hence there must exist a job J which is blocked by J_j. In addition, J's priority must be higher than or equal to that of job J_i. We now show the contradiction that J cannot be blocked by J_j. Since job J_i preempts the critical section $z_{j,n}$ of job J_j and enters its own critical section $z_{i,m}$, job J_i's priority must be higher than the priority ceilings of all the semaphores currently locked by job J_j. Since J's priority is assumed to be higher than or equal to that of J_i, it follows that job J's priority is also higher than the priority ceilings of all the semaphores currently locked by job J_j. By Lemma 2-7, J cannot be blocked by J_j. Hence the contradiction and the Lemma follows.

Definition: Transitive blocking is said to occur if a job J is blocked by J_i which, in turn, is blocked by another job J_j.

Lemma 2-9: The priority ceiling protocol prevents transitive blocking.

Proof: Suppose that transitive blocking is possible. Let J_3 block job J_2 and let job J_2 block job J_1. By the transitivity of the protocol, job J_3 will inherit the priority of J_1 which is assumed to be higher than that of job J_2. This contradicts Lemma 2-8, which shows that J_3 cannot inherit a priority that is higher than or equal to that of job J_2. The Lemma follows.

Theorem 2-10: The priority ceiling protocol prevents deadlocks.

Proof: First, by assumption, a job cannot deadlock with itself. Thus, a deadlock can only be formed by a cycle of jobs waiting for each other. Let the n jobs involved in the blocking cycle be $\{J_1, \cdots, J_n\}$. Note that each of these n jobs must be in one of its critical sections, since a job that does not hold a lock on any semaphore cannot contribute to the deadlock. By Lemma 2-9, the number of jobs in the blocking cycle can only be two, i.e., n = 2. Suppose that job J_2's critical section was preempted by job J_1, which then enters its own critical section. By Lemma 2-8, job J_2 can never inherit a priority which is higher than or equal to that of job J_1 before job J_1 completes. However, if a blocking cycle (deadlock) is formed, then by the transitivity of priority inheritance, job J_2 will inherit the priority of job J_1. This contradicts Lemma 2-8 and hence the Theorem.

Remark: Suppose that the run-time system supports PCP. Theorem 2-10 leads to the useful result that programmers can write arbitrary sequences of properly nested semaphore accesses. As long as each job does not deadlock with itself, there will be no deadlock in the system.

Lemma 2-11: Let J_L be a job with a lower priority than that of job J_i. Job J_i can be blocked by job J_L for at most the duration of one critical section in $\beta_{i,L}^*$.

Proof: First, job J_i will preempt J_L if J_L is not in a critical section $z_{L,k} \notin \beta_{i,L}^*$. Suppose that job J_i is blocked by $z_{L,k}$. By

Theorem 2-10, there is no deadlock and hence job J_L will exit $z_{L,k}$ at some instant t_1. Once job J_L leaves this critical section at time t_1, job J_L can no longer block job J_i. This is because job J_i has been initiated and J_L is not within a critical section in $\beta^*_{i,L}$. It follows from Lemma 2-1 that job J_L can no longer block job J_i.

Theorem 2-12: A job J can be blocked for at most the duration of at most one element of β^*_i.

Proof: Suppose that job J can be blocked by $n > 1$ elements of β_i By Lemma 2-11, the only possibility is that job J is blocked by n different lower priority jobs. Suppose that the first two lower priority jobs that block job J are J_1 and J_2. By Lemma 2-1, in order for both these jobs to block job J, both of them must be in a longest blocking critical section when job J is initiated. Let the lowest priority job J_2 enter its blocking critical section first, and let the highest priority ceiling of all the semaphores locked by J_2 be ρ_2. Under PCP, in order for job J_1 to enter its critical section when J_2 is already inside one, the priority of job J_1 must be higher than priority ceiling ρ_2. Since we assume that job J can be blocked by job J_2, by Lemma 2-7 the priority of job J cannot be higher than priority ceiling ρ_2. Since the priority of job J_1 is higher than ρ_2 and the priority of job J is no higher than ρ_2, job J_1's priority must be higher than the priority of job J. This contradicts the assumption that the priority of job J is higher than that of both J_1 and J_2. Thus, it is impossible for job J to have priority higher than both jobs J_1 and J_2 and to be blocked by both of them under PCP. The Theorem follows.

Remark: We may want to generalize the definition of a job by allowing it to suspend during its execution, for instance, to wait for I/O services to complete. The following corollary presents the upper bound on the blocking duration of a generalized job that might suspend and later resume during its execution.

Corollary 2-13: If a generalized job J suspends itself n times during its execution, it can be blocked by at most $n+1$ not necessarily distinct elements of β^*_i.

2.5 THE SEMAPHORE CONTROL PROTOCOL

The priority ceiling protocol defines the conditions under which a semaphore can be locked by a task. These conditions are sufficient to obtain the following properties. It not only minimizes the maximum priority inversion encountered by a job to the duration of execution of a single critical section of lower priority tasks but also avoids deadlocks. In this section, we shall briefly describe a priority inheritance protocol, called the *Semaphore Control Protocol* (SCP), which embeds necessary and sufficient conditions to obtain these two properties. In other words, the priority ceiling protocol condition can be unnecessarily restrictive.

As we shall see in Section 2.7, there is very little performance difference between the semaphore control protocol and the priority ceiling protocol. As a result, we limit discussions of SCP to the definition and illustration of the protocol. Readers interested in the formal proofs and other approximations for the semaphore control protocol are referred to [Rajkumar 88].

Definition: The *current critical section* of a job J refers to the outermost critical section that J has already entered.

2.5.1. Definition of the Semaphore Control Protocol

Notation: When a job J requests the lock on an *unlocked* semaphore S,

- S^* is a semaphore with the highest priority ceiling locked by jobs with lower priority than J.

  There can be more than one semaphore which satisfies this condition of having the highest priority ceiling. If so, *any* one of these semaphores[5] may be chosen to be S^*.

- J^* is the job holding the lock on S^*.

- SL^* is the set of semaphores already locked by the current

---

[5]However, if two or more of these semaphores are locked by the same job J', the one locked earliest by J' can be deemed to be S^* for ease of protocol implementation. Conversely, if these semaphores have been locked by more than one distinct job, the one locked the last might be chosen as S^*. It can be shown that there can be at most two different jobs which can lock semaphores with the same priority ceiling.

critical section of job J^*.[6]

- SR^* is the set of semaphores[7] that will be locked by the current critical section of job J^*. If the current critical section of job J^* does not request any more nested semaphore locks, $SR^* = \emptyset$.

- SR is the set of semaphores that J will lock within the critical section if it is granted S. If S is not granted to J, J will be blocked and $S \in SR$ if and only if J is already within a critical section.

Remark: Note that $SL^* \cap SR^* = \emptyset$ and $SL^* \cup SR^* = $ set of semaphores that can be locked by the current critical section of J^*.

SCP selectively grants locks on unlocked semaphores to jobs and is defined as follows.

Suppose that job J requests the lock on a semaphore S. If S is locked, job J is blocked and the job J^* which holds the lock on S inherits J's priority. If S is unlocked, J is allowed to lock S if and only if *at least one* of the following conditions is true.

1. **Condition C1**: $p(J) > c(S^*)$. That is, the priority of job J is greater than the priority ceiling of S^*.

2. **Condition C2**: $(p(J) = c(S^*)) \wedge (SR \cap SL^* = \emptyset)$. That is, the priority of job J is equal to the priority ceiling of S^*, and the critical section of J will not attempt to lock any semaphore already locked by J^*.

3. **Condition C3**: $(p(J) = c(S)) \wedge (S \notin SR^*)$. That is, the priority of job J is equal to the priority ceiling of S, and the lock on semaphore S will not be requested by J^*'s preempted critical section.

If none of these conditions is true, job J is blocked and J^* inherits J's priority.

We refer to conditions C1, C2 and C3 as the *locking conditions*.

---

[6]SL stands for "semaphores locked".

[7]SR stands for "semaphores required" for completion of the current critical section.

Under SCP, as under the priority ceiling protocol, a job can be blocked for the duration of at most a single critical section, and deadlocks cannot occur. We illustrate the protocol by first applying SCP to the examples in the previous section where multiple blocking occurs for a job.

Example 2.5: A job J_1 needs to lock S_1 and S_2 sequentially, while J_2 needs to lock S_1, and J_3 needs to lock S_2. Hence, $c(S_1)=c(S_2)=p(J_1)$. At time t_0, J_3 locks S_2. At time t_1, J_2 preempts J_3 and later attempts to lock S_1. Now, $J^*=J_3$ and $S^*=S_2$. However, $p(J) < c(S_2)$ and $p(J) < c(S_1)$, so all the three locking conditions are false. Hence, J_2 is blocked and J_3 inherits J_2's priority. Let J_1 arrive and attempt to lock S_1. Since J_1 does not make any nested requests for semaphore locks, we have $SR=\varnothing$ and condition C2 is true. Hence J_1 can obtain the lock on S_1. Later, when J_1 attempts to lock the locked semaphore S_2, J_3 inherits J_1's priority. When J_3 releases S_2, it resumes its original priority, and J_1 locks S_2. J_1 now runs to completion followed by J_2 and J_3 respectively.

It can be seen that both jobs J_1 and J_2 had to wait for a lower priority job J_3 for at most the duration of a single critical section guarded by S_2. The blocking encountered by J_1, when it needs semaphore S_2 locked by another job, is direct blocking. However, J_2 is blocked when J_3 inherits a priority higher than J_2. This type of blocking is push-through blocking, which is essential to avoid multiple blocking as illustrated in Example 2.5, and to avoid the uncontrolled priority inversion problem exhibited in Example 2.1.

Example 2.6: Consider the previous example where deadlocks could occur under the basic priority inheritance protocol. Job J_2 locks the semaphore S_2 and before it makes a nested request for semaphore S_1, J_1 arrives and preempts J_2. We again have $c(S_1)=c(S_2)=p(J_1)$. However, when J_1 attempts to lock S_1, we have $S^*=S_2$, $S=S_1$, $J^*=J_2$ and $p(J)=c(S^*)=c(S)$ but $SR=\{S_2\}$, $SL^*=\{S_2\}$, $SR^*=\{S_1\}$ and $S=S_1$ such that all locking conditions are false. Hence, the lock on S_1 is denied to J_1 and J_2 inherits J_1's priority. Thus, the deadlock is avoided.

We now provide an example that illustrates each of the locking conditions of SCP.

Example 2.7: Consider 5 jobs J_0, J_{1a}, J_{1b}, J_2 and J_3 in descending order of priority except that jobs J_{1a} and J_{1b} have equal priorities. There are three semaphores S_1, S_2 and S_3 in the system. Suppose the sequence of processing steps for each job is as follows:

$$J_0 = \{ \cdots, \mathbf{P}(S_0), \cdots, \mathbf{V}(S_0), \cdots \}$$

$$J_{1a} = \{ \cdots, \mathbf{P}(S_0), \cdots, \mathbf{V}(S_0), \cdots \}$$

$$J_{1b} = \{ \cdots, \mathbf{P}(S_1), \cdots, \mathbf{V}(S_1), \cdots \}$$

$$J_2 = \{ \cdots, \mathbf{P}(S_2), \cdots, \mathbf{P}(S_1), \cdots, \mathbf{V}(S_1), \cdots, \mathbf{V}(S_2), \cdots \}$$

$$J_3 = \{ \cdots, \mathbf{P}(S_1), \cdots, \mathbf{V}(S_1), \cdots, \mathbf{P}(S_2), \cdots, \mathbf{V}(S_2), \cdots \}$$

Thus, $c(S_0) = p(J_0)$, $c(S_1) = p(J_{1b}) = p(J_{1a})$, and $c(S_2) = p(J_2)$.

The sequence of events described below is depicted in Figure 2-3. Suppose that

- At time t_0, J_3 arrives and begins execution.
- At time t_1, J_3 locks the unlocked semaphore S_1 since there is no other semaphore locked by another job.[8]
- At time t_2, J_2 arrives and preempts J_3.
- At time t_3, J_2 attempts to lock S_2. Since $p(J_2) < c(S_1)$, conditions C1 and C2 are false. But, $p(J_2) = c(S_2)$ and $SR^* = \emptyset$. Hence, condition C3 is true and J_2 is allowed to lock S_2.
- At time t_4, J_0 arrives and preempts J_2.
- At time t_5, J_0 attempts to lock S_0. Now, $S^* = S_1$. However, $p(J_0) > c(S_1)$ and condition C1 is true. Hence, J_0 is granted the lock on S_0.

---

[8]The situation when no semaphores have been locked by other jobs can be treated as follows. The idle process is considered to have locked a dummy semaphore S_0 and $p(J_3) > c(S_0)$ by definition.

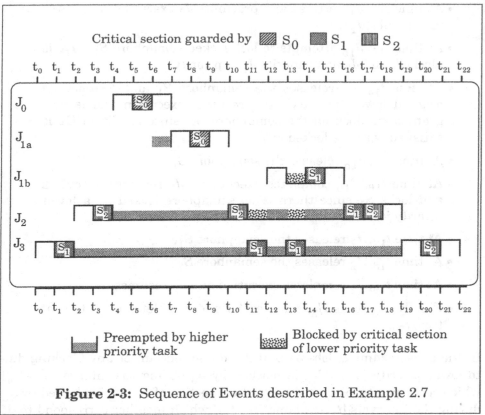

Critical section guarded by S_0 S_1 S_2

Figure 2-3: Sequence of Events described in Example 2.7

- At time t_6, J_0 releases the semaphore S_0. J_{1a} arrives now but is unable to preempt J_0.

- At time t_7, J_0 completes execution. J_{1a}, which is eligible to execute, begins execution.

- At time t_8, J_{1a} tries to lock S_0, and we have $S^* = S_1$. We have $p(J_{1a}) = c(S_1)$ and there is no nested request for semaphore locks. Hence condition C2 is true, and the lock on S_0 is granted to J_{1a}.

- At time t_9, J_{1a} releases the semaphore S_0.

- At time t_{10}, J_{1a} completes execution and J_2 resumes execution.

- At time t_{11}, J_2 attempts to lock the locked semaphore S_1 and is blocked. J_3, which holds the lock on S_1, inherits J_2's priority and resumes execution.

- At time t_{12}, J_{1b} arrives and preempts J_3 executing at a lower priority of $p(J_2)$.

- At time t_{13}, J_{1b} attempts to lock locked semaphore S_1. J_{1b} is blocked, and J_3 now inherits J_{1b}'s priority.

- At time t_{14}, J_3 releases the semaphore S_1 and resumes its original lowest priority. J_{1b} resumes execution and is now granted the lock on the semaphore S_1, since condition C1 is satisfied w.r.t. S_2 locked by J_2.

- At time t_{15}, J_{1b} releases the semaphore S_1.

- At time t_{16}, J_{1b} completes execution. J_2 resumes execution and locks S_1 since there is no semaphore locked by a lower priority job.

- At time t_{17}, J_2 releases the semaphore S_1.

- At time t_{18}, J_2 releases the semaphore S_2.

- At time t_{19}, J_2 completes execution and J_3 resumes.

- Finally, J_3 locks S_2, releases S_2 and completes execution at time t_{22}.

In the above example, jobs J_0 and J_{1a} do not encounter any blocking due to lower priority jobs. J_{1b} is blocked by J_3 during the interval $[t_{13}\text{-}t_{14}]$ which corresponds to at most one critical section of J_3. J_2 is blocked by J_3 during the intervals $[t_{11}\text{-}t_{12}]$ and $[t_{13}\text{-}t_{14}]$ which together correspond to at most one critical section of J_3.

2.6 SCHEDULABILITY ANALYSIS OF PRIORITY IN-HERITANCE PROTOCOLS

The priority inheritance protocols place an upper bound on the duration that a job can be blocked. This property makes possible the schedulability analysis of a task set using rate-monotonic priority assignment and any of these protocols. We now proceed to investigate the effect of blocking on the schedulability of a task set. In this section, we develop a set of *sufficient* conditions under which a set of periodic tasks using a priority inheritance protocol can be scheduled by the rate-monotonic algorithm [Liu 73]. To this end, we will use a simplified scheduling model. First, we assume that all the tasks are periodic. An aperiodic task can be converted to a periodic task by the use of a periodic server task and buffering the arriving aperiodic jobs. Secondly, we assume that each job of a periodic task has worst-case execution times for both its critical and non-critical sections. Readers who are interested in more general scheduling issues, such as the reduction of aperiodic response times are referred to [Lehoczky 87a]. In the present context, we assume that periodic tasks are scheduled by the rate-monotonic algorithm, which assigns a higher priority to a task with a shorter period.

We quote the following theorem due to Liu and Layland [Liu 73] which was proved under the assumption of independent tasks, i.e. when there is no blocking due to data sharing and synchronization.

Theorem 2-14: A set of n periodic tasks scheduled by the rate-monotonic algorithm can always meet their deadlines if

$$\frac{C_1}{T_1} + \cdots + \frac{C_n}{T_n} \le n(2^{1/n}-1)$$

where C_i and T_i are the execution time and period of task τ_i respectively.

Theorem 2-14 offers a sufficient (worst-case) condition that characterizes the rate-monotonic schedulability of a given periodic task set. The following exact characterization was proved by Lehoczky, Sha and Ding [Lehoczky 89]. An example of the use of this theorem will be given later in this section.

Theorem 2-15: A set of n periodic tasks scheduled by the rate-monotonic algorithm will meet all their deadlines for all task phasings if and only if

$$\forall i, \ 1 \le i \le n, \quad \min_{(k,\, l) \in R_i} \sum_{j=1}^{i} C_j \frac{1}{lT_k} \lceil \frac{lT_k}{T_j} \rceil = \min_{(k,\, l) \in R_i} \sum_{j=1}^{i} U_j \frac{T_j}{lT_k} \lceil \frac{lT_k}{T_j} \rceil \le 1$$

where C_j, T_j and U_j are the execution time, period and utilization of task τ_j respectively and $R_i = \{ (k,\, l) \mid 1 \le k \le i, \ l = 1, \cdots, \lfloor T_i/T_k \rfloor \}$.

The above exact characterization is based upon the concept of a *critical zone* for a periodic task. The phasing of a task when it has the worst response time is called its *critical instant* [Liu 73]. In the case of periodic tasks, the critical instant of a task occurs when it arrives simultaneously with all higher priority tasks. If a periodic task meets its deadline during the critical instant, it is guaranteed to meet all its deadlines. The interval between a task's critical instant and its completion is referred to as its *critical zone*.

When tasks are independent of one another, Theorems 2-14 and 2-15 provide us with the conditions under which a set of *n* periodic tasks can be scheduled by the rate-monotonic algorithm. Although these two theorems have taken into account the effect of a task being preempted by higher priority tasks, they have not considered the effect of a job being blocked due to resource-sharing requirements. We now consider the effect of blocking.

2.6.1. The Impact of Priority Inversion on Schedulability

Theorems 2-14 and 2-15 can be generalized in a straightforward fashion to take into account the duration of blocking for each task. In order to test the schedulability of τ_i, we need to consider the preemptions caused by higher priority tasks, its own utilization and the maximum blocking duration that it can encounter. We denote the worst-case blocking time of a job in task τ_i by B_i. That is, the blocking of any job of τ_i can be in the form of direct blocking, push-through blocking, ceiling blocking or any other form of blocking but does not exceed B_i. Then, Theorem 2-14 becomes

> **Theorem 2-16:** A set of n periodic tasks sharing resources can be scheduled by the rate monotonic algorithm if the following conditions are satisfied:
>
> $$\forall\, i,\ 1 \le i \le n,\quad \frac{C_1}{T_1} + \frac{C_2}{T_2} + \cdots + \frac{C_i}{T_i} + \frac{B_i}{T_i} \le i(2^{1/i} - 1).$$

Proof: Suppose that for each task τ_i the inequality is satisfied. It follows that the inequality of Theorem 2-14 will also be satisfied with $n = i$ and C_i replaced by $C_i^* = (C_i + B_i)$. That is, in the absence of blocking, any job of task τ_i will still meet its deadline even if it executes for $(C_i + B_i)$ units of time. It follows that task τ_i, if it executes for only C_i units of time, can be delayed by

B_i units of time and still meet its deadline. Hence the theorem follows.

<u>Remark</u>: The first i terms in the above inequality constitute the effect of preemptions from all higher priority tasks and τ_i's own execution time, while B_i of the last term represents the worst-case blocking time of task τ_i due to all sources including all lower priority tasks. To illustrate the effect of blocking in Theorem 2-16, suppose that we have three harmonic tasks:

$$\tau_1 = (C_1 = 1, T_1 = 2)$$
$$\tau_2 = (C_2 = 1, T_2 = 4)$$
$$\tau_3 = (C_3 = 2, T_3 = 8)$$

In addition, $B_1 = B_2 = 1$. Since these tasks are harmonic, the utilization bound becomes 100%. Thus, we have "$C_1/T_1 + B_1/T_1 = 1$" for task τ_1. Next, we have "$C_1/T_1 + C_2/T_2 + B_2/T_2 = 1$" for task τ_2. Finally, we have "$C_1/T_1 + C_2/T_2 + C_3/T_3 = 1$" for task τ_3. Since all three inequalities hold, these three tasks can meet all their deadlines.

Corollary 2-17: A set of n periodic tasks sharing resources can be scheduled by the rate monotonic algorithm if the following condition is satisfied:

$$\frac{C_1}{T_1} + \cdots + \frac{C_n}{T_n} + max(\frac{B_1}{T_1}, \cdots, \frac{B_{n-1}}{T_{n-1}}) \leq n(2^{1/n}-1)$$

Proof: Since $n(2^{1/n}-1) \leq i(2^{1/i}-1)$ and $max(\frac{B_1}{T_1}, \cdots, \frac{B_{n-1}}{T_{n-1}}) \geq \frac{B_i}{T_i}$, if this inequality holds then all the inequalities in Theorem 2-16 also hold.

Similar to the sufficient condition in Theorem 2-16, the conditions in Theorem 2-15 can be easily generalized. Specifically,

Theorem 2-18: A set of n periodic tasks sharing resources can be scheduled by the rate-monotonic algorithm for all task phasings if

$$\forall i, 1 \leq i \leq n, \quad \min_{(k, l) \in R_i} [\sum_{j=1}^{i-1} U_j \frac{T_j}{lT_k} \lceil \frac{lT_k}{T_j} \rceil + \frac{C_i}{lT_k} + \frac{B_i}{lT_k}] \leq 1$$

where R_i, C_i, T_i and U_i are defined in Theorem 2-15, and B_i is the worst-case blocking time for τ_i.

Proof: The proof is identical to that of Theorem 2-16.

<u>Remark</u>: The blocking duration B_i represents the worst-case conditions and hence the necessary and sufficient conditions of Theorem 2-15 become sufficient conditions in Theorem 2-18.

The following example helps clarify the use of Theorem 2-18. Consider the case of three periodic tasks:

- Task τ_1: $C_1 = 40$; $T_1 = 100$; $B_1 = 20$; $U_1 = 0.4$
- Task τ_2: $C_2 = 40$; $T_2 = 150$; $B_2 = 30$; $U_2 = 0.267$
- Task τ_3: $C_3 = 100$; $T_3 = 350$; $B_3 = 0$; $U_3 = 0.286$

Task τ_1 can be blocked by task τ_2 for at most 20 units, while τ_2 can be blocked by task τ_3 for at most 30 time-units. The lowest priority task, τ_3 cannot be blocked by any lower priority tasks. The total utilization of the task set ignoring blocking is 0.952, far too large to apply the conditions of Theorem 2-16. Theorem 2-18 is checked as follows:

1. Task τ_1: Check $C_1 + B_1 \leq 100$. Since $40 + 20 \leq 100$, task τ_1 is schedulable.

2. Task τ_2: Check whether either

$$C_1 + C_2 + B_2 \leq 100 \qquad 80 + 30 > 100$$
$$\text{or} \quad 2C_1 + C_2 + B_2 \leq 150 \qquad 120 + 30 \leq 150$$

Task τ_2 is schedulable and in the worst-case phasing will meet its deadline exactly at time 150.

3. Task τ_3: Check whether either

$$C_1 + C_2 + C_3 \leq 100 \qquad 40 + 40 + 100 > 100$$

$$\text{or} \quad 2C_1 + C_2 + C_3 \leq 150 \qquad 80 + 40 + 100 > 150$$

$$\text{or} \quad 2C_1 + 2C_2 + C_3 \leq 200 \qquad 80 + 80 + 100 > 200$$

$$\text{or} \quad 3C_1 + 2C_2 + C_3 \leq 300 \qquad 120 + 80 + 100 = 300$$

$$\text{or} \quad 4C_1 + 3C_2 + C_3 \leq 350 \qquad 160 + 120 + 100 > 350$$

Task τ_3 is also schedulable and in the worst-case phasing will meet its deadline exactly at time 300.

Theorems 2-16 and 2-18 require the determination of B_i for each task τ_i. It must be remembered that B_i is finite and known only when one uses a synchronization protocol that avoids the unbounded priority inversion problem and bounds the duration of priority inversion. Since the priority inheritance protocols exhibit these properties, Theorems 2-16 and 2-18 can be used to determine the schedulability of a task set using any of these protocols. The determination of B_i for the basic inheritance protocol, PCP and SCP are described below.

2.6.2. Determination of B_i for SCP

<u>Definition</u>: Jobs J_i and J_j are said to be *active* together, if J_i and J_j can both be ready to execute on the processor at some instant in time.

For instance, in Example 2.7, jobs J_2 and J_3 are said to be active together since both are ready to execute at time t_1. However, jobs J_{1a} and J_{1b}, in reality, can be the execution of a single instance of task τ_1 with an intervening suspension (say for communication or I/O activities). That is, job J_1 actually consists of two jobs J_{1a} and J_{1b}. Since J_{1a} always precedes job J_{1b}, jobs J_{1a} and J_{1b} are said to be *not* active together.

The value of B_i for each task τ_i when SCP is used is computed as follows. A job J_i can be *blocked* only by jobs with lower priority. A critical section z_j of a lower priority job J_j guarded by a semaphore $S_{j,k}$ can block J_i if

- $p(J_i) < c(S_{j,k})$

  OR

- $p(J_i) = c(S_{j,k}) \wedge J_i$ (or an equal priority job that is active with J_i) may lock $S_{j,k}$.

Hence, each element in $\beta_{i,j}$ is a critical section of J_j that meets one of the above two conditions. The set of maximal elements of $\beta_{i,j}$, $\beta_{i,j}^*$, is formed by eliminating those critical sections nested inside other elements of $\beta_{i,j}$. Then, B_i is equal to the length of the longest critical section in $\beta_i^* = \cup_{j>i} \beta_{i,j}^*$, the set of all outermost critical sections that can block J_i.

2.6.3. Determination of B_i for PCP

The determination of B_i for each task τ_i under the PCP proceeds as follows. Each element in β_i is a critical section accessed by a lower priority job and guarded by a semaphore whose priority ceiling is higher than or equal to the priority of job J_i. Hence, β_i^* can be derived from β_i. By Lemma 2-7 and Theorem 2-12, job J_i of a task τ can be blocked for at most the duration of a single element in β_i^*. Hence the worst-case blocking time for J is at most the duration of the longest element of β_i^*. Again, given a set of n periodic tasks, $B_n = 0$, since there is no lower priority task to block τ_n.

Actually, if no jobs (voluntarily) suspend themselves during execution, the conditions to determine B_i for SCP are identical to the blocking conditions for PCP, and the worst-case blocking times would be identical under PCP and SCP. However, if job J_i does suspend n times, B_i would be $n+1$ times the maximum blocking duration if J were not to suspend at all. Under the SCP, the blocking duration may not necessarily be scaled $n+1$ times. As a result, it is possible that SCP can yield a better guaranteed performance for certain task sets.

2.6.4. Determination of B_i for the Basic Inheritance Protocol

Since the value of B_i must be bounded and the basic protocol does not avoid deadlocks, the determination procedure applies only if deadlocks are avoided by other techniques such as partial ordering of resource accesses. The procedure to determine B_i is relatively more complicated, and interested readers are referred to Appendix A. It defines a branch-and-bound technique to determine B_i for the basic inheritance protocol under the assumption that deadlocks are avoided.

2.6.5. Extensions to the Priority Inheritance Protocols

Other extensions to the priority ceiling protocol are possible. The notion of priority ceiling of a semaphore in the priority ceiling and semaphore control protocols assumes that the priority of a task is assigned statically. The schedulability analysis of Section 2.6.1 describes how the blocking factor arising from synchronization requirements can be accounted for, when rate-monotonic scheduling is used. Chen and Lin [Chen 89] have developed a dynamic priority ceiling protocol that can be used in conjunction with the dynamic earliest deadline scheduling algorithm, the optimal scheduling algorithm on uniprocessors. In their analysis, it is possible that the blocking duration for a task under the dynamic priority ceiling protocol can be larger than that under the priority ceiling protocol. In addition, Baker [Baker 90] has shown that the blocking duration under the earliest deadline scheduling algorithm is not higher than that with rate-monotonic scheduling. Jeffay [Jeffay 89] has studied the issues of priority inheritance in the scheduling of sporadic tasks.

2.7 PERFORMANCE OF THE PRIORITY INHERITANCE PROTOCOLS

The priority inheritance protocols offer the desirable properties of analyzability and predictability in building real-time systems. However, these protocols must be easy to implement and efficient in performance to be of practical use in real systems. Among the various concerns which arise during implementation, chief are the compile-time and run-time overhead imposed, the implementation complexity, and the support available for the protocols in existing programming languages. We have already outlined the implementation of the key inheritance protocols in Sections 2.3.2 and 2.4.3. In this section, we conduct experimental studies to compare the performance of various synchronization protocols, and demonstrate that the priority inheritance protocols provide a significant advantage both in terms of guaranteed performance and actual performance.

The performance study experiments are aimed at evaluating the damaging effects of priority inversion and the superiority, if any, of the proposed synchronization protocols. This is carried out by implementing various synchronization protocols on an Ada run-time system with the Ada rendezvous acting as the synchronization mechanism, and in a simulator program.[9]

The experiments are designed to study the effects of the worst-case blocking time of a task on the actual schedulability of randomly chosen task sets. The results motivate the need for minimizing blocking durations. We determine the schedulability of task sets based on Theorem 2-18. We pick a random set of $n = 10$ tasks, each of which is characterized by $\{C_i, T_i\}$. For each task set, there exists a critical scaling factor w, which is a function of (C_i, T_i), $1 \leq i \leq n$, such that the transformed task set $\{(wC_1, T_1), \cdots, (wC_n, T_n)\}$ is just schedulable using the specified scheduling algo-

---

[9]The simulator program is written in C and runs on Unix systems.

rithm and synchronization protocol. In other words, any increase in w would cause a task deadline to be missed. The associated utilization $U_w = \sum_{i=1}^{n} \frac{wC_i}{T_i}$ is referred to as the *breakdown utilization*.

The breakdown utilization is determined for random task sets under different synchronization protocols. The model that we use is as follows: Each task τ_i on arrival executes for $C_{i,1}$ units of time, then enters a critical section for $C_{i,2}$ units of time, and then executes normally for $C_{i,3}$ units of time. Thus, $C_i = C_{i,1} + C_{i,2} + C_{i,3}$. Entry to a critical section requires the locking of a semaphore, and another critical section may be nested inside the outer critical section. If the critical section is nested, the sequence of nested semaphore locks is partially ordered to avoid deadlocks[10]. The durations of time executed before the nested critical section, within the nested critical section, and after the nested critical section are equal. Under these assumptions, a random task set is generated from uniform distributions and scheduled under different protocols. The breakdown utilization is determined in each case. A theoretical worst-case prediction is also computed if the protocol in use guarantees an upper bound to B_i. The protocols that are used include

- *The Basic Inheritance Protocol* (BIP): A task can be blocked for at most $min(m, k)$ critical sections, where m is the number of lower priority tasks and k is the number of distinct semaphores locked by lower priority tasks.

- *The Priority Ceiling Protocol* (PCP): A task τ can be blocked for at most a single critical section (guarded by a semaphore with a priority ceiling $\geq \tau$'s priority).

- *The Kernel Priority Protocol* (KPP): A task within a critical section is non-preemptable (by masking off interrupts). A task can be blocked for the duration of at most one critical section of any lower priority task.

- *The Caller Priority Protocol* (CPP/PQ, CPP/FQ): A task within a critical section executes at its own priority. *No* priority inheritance is used if another task blocks on the locked semaphore. Tasks blocked on a semaphore may be queued in either priority order (CPP/PQ) or FCFS order (CPP/FQ).

---

[10]This partial ordering of resource accesses is *not* required for PCP and its enhancements. See Section 2.7.1.

Breakdown Utilization Experiment w/ 5 semaphores					
Measure	Basic Inheritance Protocol	Priority Ceiling Protocol	Kernel Priority	Caller Priority (priority q)	Caller Priority (FIFO q)
Average Utilization w/ critical phasing	0.7934	0.8066	0.7694	0.5466	0.5498
Average Utilization w/ random phasing	0.8219	0.8345	0.7853	0.5438	0.5389
Worst Difference w.r.t. PCP	0.1621	-	0.2969	0.5283	0.5283
Worst-case Prediction	0.6462	0.7922	0.7473	0.0	0.0

Table 2-1: Breakdown Utilization for Different Protocols
with 5 Semaphores

Breakdown Utilization Experiment w/ 10 semaphores					
Measure	Basic Inheritance Protocol	Priority Ceiling Protocol	Kernel Priority	Caller Priority (priority q)	Caller Priority (FIFO q)
Average Utilization w/ critical phasing	0.8294	0.8339	0.7906	0.6320	0.6319
Average Utilization w/ random phasing	0.8723	0.8773	0.8199	0.6064	0.6064
Worst Difference w.r.t. PCP	0.0732	-	0.4795	0.4571	0.4571
Worst-case Prediction	0.7387	0.8244	0.7725	0.0	0.0

Table 2-2: Breakdown Utilization for Different Protocols
with 10 Semaphores

The breakdown utilizations for these protocols were averaged over multiple task sets and are tabulated in Table 2-1. We assume that there are 5 semaphores in the system. Three types of breakdown utilization are

Ada Run-Time Experiments					
Task Set #	PrIn w/FIFO 68k Unix P	BIP 68k Unix P	Old Ceiling 68k Unix P	Old High 68k Unix P	Old Low 68k Unix P	PCP 68k Unix P
1	88 90 --	88 90 90	88 90 90	88 90 90	29 29 --	88 90 90
2	76 72 --	76 76 56	76 77 66	49 49 49	45 41 --	78 76 66
3	79 80 --	79 80 80	79 80 80	79 80 80	70 71 --	79 80 80
4	86 88 --	87 88 88	87 88 88	87 88 88	55 52 --	87 88 88
5	89 77 --	82 77 73	89 77 75	90 77 75	34 34 --	89 77 75
6	97 99 --	97 99 96	97 99 98	98 99 98	19 12 --	97 99 98
7	90 91 --	90 91 92	90 91 92	90 91 91	38 24 --	90 91 92
8	82 79 --	83 79 58	86 88 63	55 62 50	12 12 --	84 79 63
9	92 94 --	92 94 86	92 94 86	93 94 86	28 34 --	92 94 86
10	91 93 --	91 93 84	91 93 93	91 93 93	55 56 --	91 93 93
11	30 50 --	30 50 27	61 62 46	20 18 16	10 13 --	61 62 46
12	91 93 --	91 93 66	91 93 85	71 75 69	36 40 --	91 93 85
13	88 90 --	89 90 91	89 90 91	89 90 91	58 53 --	89 90 91
14	88 86 --	84 86 48	87 91 86	85 94 86	31 27 --	91 91 86
15	87 88 --	87 88 87	87 88 89	87 88 89	26 38 --	87 88 89
16	93 95 --	94 95 88	94 95 96	94 95 96	30 28 --	94 95 96
17	49 53 --	49 54 43	49 54 46	50 41 34	17 16 --	49 54 46
18	53 49 --	50 55 44	55 58 47	55 58 47	23 23 --	53 55 47
19	90 91 --	91 91 81	91 91 81	91 92 81	45 45 --	91 91 81
20	96 98 --	96 98 98	96 98 98	96 98 98	12 12 --	96 98 98
21	91 93 --	91 93 83	91 93 94	91 93 89	31 32 --	91 93 94
22	95 97 --	95 97 93	95 97 93	95 97 93	27 27 --	95 96 93
23	92 95 --	93 95 94	93 95 94	93 91 84	20 16 --	92 94 94
24	95 97 --	95 95 79	95 96 85	87 93 84	17 17 --	95 96 85
25	91 93 --	91 93 81	92 93 88	92 93 88	41 41 --	92 93 88
Avg. Diff. from Worst	--	9.36	4.84	3.76	--	4.24

Table 2-3: Breakdown Utilizations from Various Ada Run-Time Systems

presented: when the tasks are initiated simultaneously[11], when the tasks are initiated at random phasings, and the worst-case predictions using Theorem 2-18. As can be seen, the priority ceiling protocol yields the highest average performance, followed by the basic inheritance protocol, the kernel priority and the caller priority protocols. While BIP and KPP may seem acceptable, it must be noted that they can yield poor performance for some task sets (with a maximum loss of 16% and 29% schedulability w.r.t. PCP) and also yield poor guaranteed performance. BIP typically performs much better than the worst-case prediction since the worst case can happen only with convoluted phasings which may or may not be feasible. Some additional schedulability is obtained when the phasings between the tasks are randomized. As can be seen, the traditional use of CPP with FIFO queueing on semaphores displays very poor performance and the inclusion of a priority queue does not help either. Since there is no upper bound on the blocking duration, a worst-case prediction is also not possible. We conclude that avoiding unbounded priority inversion is essential in order to obtain both predictability and high performance. Similar results (Table 2-2) are obtained with upto 10 semaphores in the system.

Other protocols that are also of interest are the following:

- *The Ceiling Semaphore Protocol* (CSP): This is an approximation of the priority ceiling protocol, and requires the execution of each critical section guarded by a semaphore S *always* at a priority equal to the priority ceiling of S. Its guaranteed worst-case performance is identical to that of PCP. Baker [Baker 90] has shown that the ceiling semaphore protocol can be used to share the same run-time stack among all tasks. However, as we shall see in Section 2.7.1, the deadlock avoidance property of the priority ceiling protocol is slightly superior to the ceiling semaphore protocol. Also, the sharing of stacks is possible only if a task does not suspend for any I/O or communication activity before completion.

- *The Semaphore Control Protocol* (SCP): This optimal priority inheritance protocol described in Section 2.5 embeds necessary and sufficient conditions to ensure two properties: avoidance

---

[11]This phasing corresponds to the most critical phasing for independent tasks [Liu 73].

of deadlock and a worst-case blocking of at most one critical section.

The ceiling semaphore protocol and enhancements of the priority ceiling protocol (such as the semaphore control protocol) perform almost identical to PCP under the conditions of this experiment and are not listed in Tables 2-1 and 2-2.

In order to provide a better perspective of the relative performance of these synchronization protocols, we also present Table 2-3 which lists the breakdown utilization for each of 25 random task sets, where each task set comprises of 10 tasks. The protocols were implemented in an Ada run-time system, and a pseudo-application emulating each of these task sets was run under different run-time systems implementing these various protocols. The protocols were actually implemented and tested on a Unix-based system (where the Ada run-time system runs on top of Unix), and a 68020-based single-board computer where the Ada run-time system runs on top of the bare hardware. The third column under each protocol lists the worst-case breakdown utilization predicted by the protocol in use. The last row lists the average difference between the predicted worst-case performance and the actual higher performance obtained. The entry "--" is marked against protocols which do not guarantee any worst-case performance. The timing requirements for each task set were scaled up such that the run-time overhead for each of these protocols is masked out. However, it must be emphasized that the implementation of PCP and BIP in a commercial Ada run-time system was relatively simple and actually streamlined the original implementation with the removal of some queues and checks.

In Ada, each critical region is protected by a server task with multiple entries. Each client task requiring entry into the region makes an entry call to one of these entries, and executes the critical region code within the rendezvous. The server task can be assigned its own independent priority. If multiple tasks make entry calls to the same server task, the entry calls will be queued up for servicing. As a result, the following protocols apply to Ada. The basic inheritance and priority ceiling protocols are equivalent to their semaphore counterparts.

- *Priority Inheritance w/ FIFO entry queues*: This protocol implements priority inheritance when a task blocks on an entry call, but uses a FIFO queueing discipline on the server entry queues. The basic inheritance protocol requires the queues to be priority ordered in addition to using priority inheritance.

- *Old Ceiling*: This protocol utilizes the existing Ada run-time system without any changes but assigns to each server task (semaphore) a priority equal to its priority ceiling. This is the Ada implementation of the Ceiling Semaphore Protocol.

- *Old High*: This protocol again utilizes the existing Ada run-time system with each server task being assigned a priority higher than any client task. Thus, this protocol acts as the Ada implementation of the Kernel Semaphore protocol.

- *Old Low*: This protocol uses the existing Ada run-time system but assigns to each server task a priority lower than any client task. Such a protocol can be thought of to be unique to Ada, since in a semaphore implementation, a critical section will be executed at least at the priority of the caller.

The results are qualitatively similar to those listed in Table 2-2. The only new (perhaps obvious) result is that the Old Low Priority Server protocol performs relatively miserably.

2.7.1. Deadlock Avoidance

The synchronization protocols presented in the previous section vary in their ability to avoid mutual deadlocks in the system when critical sections are nested. These properties are listed in Table 2-10. Some protocols avoid deadlocks only if they are not allowed to suspend within a critical section. A task may suspend within a critical section, say, for communication or I/O purposes.

When protocols that do not exhibit the mutual deadlock avoidance property are used, other explicit deadlock avoidance techniques like partial ordering of resource accesses must be used. Such techniques are not required for the priority ceiling protocol and the semaphore control protocol.

2.7.2. Protocol Comparison Under Transient Overloads

In this section, we compare the performance of the protocols under transient overload conditions. In these experiments, we fix the utilization of a randomly chosen task set at overloaded levels and count the number of

Deadlock Avoidance Properties of Protocols	
Protocol	Deadlock avoidance property
Basic Inheritance Protocol	Does not avoid mutual deadlock.
Priority Ceiling Protocol	Avoids mutual deadlock.
Semaphore Control Protocol	Avoids mutual deadlock.
Ceiling Semaphore Protocol	Avoids mutual deadlock only if task cannot suspend within a critical section.
Kernel Priority Protocol	Avoids mutual deadlock only if task cannot suspend within a critical section.
Caller Priority Protocols	Do not avoid mutual deadlock.

Table 2-4: Deadlock Avoidance Properties of Different Protocols

deadlines missed during a hyperperiod[12]. The three highest priority tasks enter critical sections stochastically with probability 0.1. If these tasks do execute their critical sections, the total utilization of the task set is 125%. The relative performance of various protocols w.r.t. PCP is presented in Table 2-5. We again assume that there are 5 semaphores in the system. The average performance in row 1 is determined as follows: the value {(number of deadlines missed under protocol – number of deadline missed under PCP) / number of deadlines missed under PCP} * 100.0 is computed for each task set, and is averaged across multiple task sets. The second and third rows present the extremes of the performances averaged and listed in the first row. Thus, the second row represents the poorest performance of the protocols w.r.t. PCP, while the third row presents the best performance of the protocols w.r.t. PCP, when they perform better than PCP. A high value in row 2 represents poorer performance than PCP, while a low (negative) value in row 3 represents better performance than PCP.

As can be seen, PCP and SCP perform almost equally on the average, with SCP performing much better sometimes and worse sometimes. This is primarily because all the synchronization protocols are sensitive to relative task phasings. BIP has a wide range of performance, but is good on the average. In contrast, CSP no longer performs well. The principal

---

[12]The hyperperiod is the least common multiple of the periods in the task set.

Overload Performance relative to PCP w/ 5 semaphores					
Measure	Basic Inheritance Protocol	Semaphore Control Protocol	Ceiling Semaphore Protocol	Kernel Priority	Caller Priority (priority q)
Avg. difference (%)	7.64	2.68	19.88	85.46	204.98
Worst Difference (%)	87.50	43.6	88.89	290.74	631.25
Best Difference (%)	-28.57	-50.00	-33.33	-16.67	+5.00

Table 2-5: Relative Deadline Misses for Different Protocols
with 5 semaphores

Overload Performance relative to PCP w/ 10 semaphores					
Measure	Basic Inheritance Protocol	Semaphore Control Protocol	Ceiling Semaphore Protocol	Kernel Priority	Caller Priority (priority q)
Avg. difference (%)	9.29	6.06	24.64	203.03	194.74
Worst Difference (%)	42.85	40.00	157.14	1177.77	671.42
Best Difference (%)	34.14	12.50	7.14	7.69	0.00

Table 2-6: Deadline Misses for Different Protocols w/ 10 semaphores

reason is that the priority ceilings of semaphores under these conditions
have high values very rarely, while CSP assumes that these priority ceilings are high all the time. KPP performs badly most of the time, while
CPP performs dismally even with priority queues. As shown in Table 2-6,
an identical situation persists when there are 10 semaphores in the system.

2.7.3. Summary of Results of Experimental Studies

Our experiments lead us to the following conclusions. It is imperative that unbounded priority inversion be avoided in real-time systems. The inclusion of priority queues on semaphores without support for some type of priority inheritance does not help. The basic inheritance protocol, which uses only run-time information about tasks, performs acceptably well, but the theoretically guaranteed performance levels may not always be satisfactory. The performance of kernelized monitors falls within acceptable limits on the average but it may be extremely unsuitable for some task sets. The priority ceiling protocol, its approximation (the ceiling semaphore protocol) and its enhancements (such as the semaphore control protocol) provide similar performance under simple conditions. Since CSP does not avoid deadlocks under all conditions, its use must be limited to systems where this does not pose a problem. Else, other techniques must be used to avoid deadlocks. Under overloaded conditions, the priority ceiling and the semaphore control protocols perform best on average, with their relative performance depending upon the nature of the task set. The semaphore control protocol, however, can provide a slightly higher guaranteed schedulable level for some task sets. When the absolute worst-case performance is important, one might consider implementing this protocol. The ceiling semaphore protocol and the kernel priority protocols do not perform well under overloaded conditions. The basic inheritance protocol has a wide range of performance under these conditions. In contrast, the priority ceiling protocol performs well under almost all conditions.

2.8 SUMMARY

Priority inversion cannot be eliminated from a practical real-time system due to synchronization and mutual exclusion requirements. However, it is essential that the synchronization primitives used in real-time systems should bound the duration of priority inversion that a job can encounter. Only then can the deadlines of jobs be guaranteed. In addition, the duration of priority inversion must be minimized so that jobs can meet their deadlines at high levels of processor utilization. A direct application of commonly used primitives like semaphores, monitors and Ada rendezvous can, unfortunately, lead to unbounded priority inversion, where a high priority job can be blocked by a lower priority job for an arbitrary amount of time.

Priority inheritance protocols solve this unbounded priority inversion problem, and bound the blocking duration that a job can experience. We have presented an entire family of protocols based on the concept of priority inheritance, and have investigated the properties of three important members of this protocol family: the basic inheritance protocol, the priority ceiling protocol and the semaphore control protocol. Under the basic inheritance protocol, the unbounded priority inversion problem is avoided, but still deadlocks can occur and a job can encounter a long duration of priority inversion. The priority ceiling protocol allows semaphores to be locked selectively. As a result, under the priority ceiling protocol, deadlocks are avoided and a job can encounter priority inversion for at most the duration of a single critical section. While these properties of the priority ceiling protocol are very attractive, the protocol is unnecessarily restrictive disallowing certain semaphore locks from being granted. The semaphore control protocol is an optimal priority inheritance protocol in the sense that it embeds necessary and sufficient conditions under which a semaphore can be locked but still achieve these two properties. This protocol is also optimal in the sense that no other priority inheritance protocol can guarantee a better worst-case duration of priority inversion for a job.

The basic inheritance and priority ceiling protocols can be easily implemented. Experimental studies show that the priority inheritance protocols provide better guaranteed and actual performance under worst-case conditions, in avoiding deadlocks, and under transient overload conditions. In particular, the priority ceiling protocol performs well over a wide range of conditions and is also attractive due to its simplicity.

Chapter Three

Synchronization in Multiple Processor Systems

3.1 INTRODUCTION

The potential speedup provided by multiprocessors and distributed systems has motivated their widespread use in recent years. Several mechanisms exist to synchronize tasks that execute on different processors, but share data and resources. In a hard real-time context, however, these synchronization mechanisms need to have bounded blocking durations. Only then can the deadlines of tasks be guaranteed. Unfortunately, as illustrated in Chapter 2, a direct application of commonly used synchronization primitives like semaphores, monitors or message-passing mechanisms such as the Ada rendezvous can lead to uncontrolled priority inversion where a higher priority task is blocked by a lower priority task for an indefinite period of time. This chapter studies the class of *priority inheritance protocols* for synchronizing tasks executing in parallel on multiple processors. The *distributed priority ceiling protocol* and the *multiprocessor priority ceiling protocol* are priority inheritance protocols for use in distributed systems and shared memory multiprocessors respectively. Both protocols not only bound the duration of blocking but also prevent deadlocks. These properties allow us to derive a set of sufficient conditions under which a set of periodic tasks using one of these protocols will be schedulable.

The priority inheritance protocols developed in Chapter 2 constitute priority management schemes for synchronization primitives which remedy the uncontrolled priority inversion problem on uniprocessors. In this chapter, we extend these protocols to multiple processor systems with and without shared memory. We formally define the protocols in a multiple processor environment and in terms of binary semaphores. Section 3.2 discusses the issues of scheduling analysis and resource sharing that arise when we move from the uniprocessor domain to multiple processor systems. Section 3.3 presents the *distributed processor priority ceiling protocol* for distributed systems with no shared memory and analyzes its properties. Section 3.4 outlines a task allocation scheme based on the protocol. Section 3.5 presents the *multiprocessor priority ceiling protocol* for shared memory multiprocessor systems and analyzes its properties. Finally, Section 3.6 presents a brief summary of our results.

Recall from Section 2.7 that the priority ceiling protocol performs as well as the semaphore control protocol except under some transient overload conditions. In addition, PCP can be implemented with relative ease, and both the compile-time information and the run-time execution to implement the protocol can be efficiently generated and used. As a result, we concentrate only on the priority ceiling protocol in extending the priority inheritance protocols to multiprocessor and distributed systems. We shall adopt the same strategy in Chapter 4 for distributed real-time databases as well. In this chapter, we shall use the term "multiple processor systems" when the discussion applies to both distributed and shared memory multiprocessor systems.

3.2 SYNCHRONIZATION IN MULTIPLE PROCESSOR SYSTEMS

We now consider some basic synchronization issues in real-time multiple processor systems. We identify the multiprocessor and distributed system configurations that we consider, and study the trade-off between binding tasks to processors statically and dynamically. We then introduce the concept of remote blocking, and define the objectives of a synchronization protocol for multiple processor real-time systems. Finally, we state some of the assumptions that have been made throughout this chapter.

3.2.1. Typical System Configuration

A typical example of a multiple processor configuration in which this protocol can be used is presented in Figure 3-1. We consider a configuration with multiple processors connected together by a communication network like a LAN or a backplane bus. If the communication medium is indeed a bus (or similar medium with low latency[13]), shared memory

---

[13]Examples of other low latency media are hierarchical bus structures and interprocessor networks such as multi-stage switching networks.

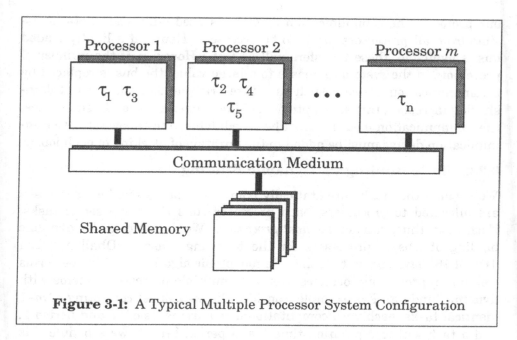

Figure 3-1: A Typical Multiple Processor System Configuration

module(s) may also be present in the system, and the configuration would be considered a multiprocessor. If it is a high latency communication medium such as a token ring, shared memory modules are not present, and we consider it a distributed system. We develop two protocols in this chapter, one for use in shared memory multiprocessors, and the other for use in distributed systems. It is, of course, possible to use the distributed synchronization protocol in shared memory systems as well.

The system configuration shown in Figure 3-1 also depicts specific tasks running on particular processors. For instance, tasks τ_1 and τ_3 are bound to processor $\wp_1$, tasks τ_2, τ_4 and τ_5 to processor $\wp_2$, and task τ_n to processor $\wp_m$. This feature illustrates a dominant characteristic of our approach where tasks are statically bound to processors, i.e. they do not migrate from one processor to another. The rationale behind this design choice will be discussed shortly. The analysis of our protocol also assumes that the delay to communicate between processors is negligible compared to task execution times.[14] This assumption is partly justified in that under

---

[14]In an ideal configuration, point-to-point connections between processors would be available, and the assumption would be true.

our protocols the communication medium is used only when data accessible from all processors needs to be accessed. Hence, if a lightly loaded bus is available, these transfers will be fast. However, if the number of processors in the system increases to a large value, the bus is replaced by a communication network such as a token-ring, and/or the level of data-sharing increases, this assumption would no longer be true. In such cases, the communication medium must be schedulable, and the worst-case communication delays must be added to the duration of blocking of each job.

3.2.2. Static Binding vs. Dynamic Binding

We assume that tasks are statically bound to a processor, i.e. once tasks are allocated to processors, each processor runs the same set of tasks. Each task, thus, runs on its *host processor*. We do not consider dynamic binding of jobs to processors for the following reason. Dhall and Liu [Dhall 78] have shown that the rate-monotonic algorithm, which performs well on uniprocessors, behaves poorly for multiple processor systems with dynamic binding. For example, consider the m-task set consisting of $m-1$ identical tasks, each with computational requirements of 2ε and period 1, and a task with computation time 1 and period $1+\varepsilon$. If we schedule this set of tasks on an $m-1$ processor system with dynamic binding, the highest priority $m-1$ tasks ready to run are scheduled on the $m-1$ processors. However, the first job of the task with period $1+\varepsilon$ will miss its deadline. The utilization factor of this task set is $U=2(m-1)\varepsilon+1/(1+\varepsilon)$. As $\varepsilon\to 0$, $U\to 1$, i.e. a deadline can be missed with just $1/m-1$ of the available processor cycles being utilized. In contrast, with static binding, the task with period $1+\varepsilon$ can be bound to a dedicated processor and the other tasks statically bound to a different processor. The task set becomes schedulable with merely two processors. In general, with static binding, *each* processor can be utilized at least upto ln 2 (69%), the least upper bound of schedulable utilization when the rate-monotonic scheduling algorithm is used. An identical situation exists for dynamic priority scheduling algorithms such as the earliest deadline scheduling algorithm as well. Dynamic binding, in principle, could give better performance if certain combinations of task bindings are not allowed to occur, e.g. the above worst-case situation must be detected and avoided during run-time. Without sophisticated run-time evaluation, such bad combinations could be realized. In real-time systems, we typically cannot perform such combinatorial analyses during run-time, and a static solution is preferable.

It must be emphasized that the decision to use static binding of tasks to processors is made independent of any synchronization requirements. The analysis of dynamic binding, when possible, is complex and can lead to poor utilization even without the introduction of synchronization constraints. Thus, the rationale behind this approach is two-fold. First and foremost, we choose static binding over dynamic binding to obtain acceptable schedulable utilization when there is no resource-sharing. Only then are synchronization requirements introduced and the need to design an appropriate synchronization protocol arises.

3.2.3. The Concept of Remote Blocking

In an ideal priority-based preemptive scheduling environment on a uniprocessor, a task only waits for equal priority tasks that arrive earlier or for higher priority tasks. As described in Chapter 2, however, the need for synchronizing accesses to shared resources can also force a task to wait for lower priority tasks. This gives rise to priority inversion, and we defined *blocking* as the duration that a job has to wait for the execution of lower priority tasks. This notion of waiting or blocking time is a fundamental concept in the schedulability analysis. Alternatively, the *blocking* time of a task can be defined as the duration that a task has to wait additionally relative to the situation where there is no resource-sharing. That is, if there were no sharing of resources, a task would not be blocked. With resource-sharing, a task may be forced to wait to access a resource, and its waiting time for lower priority tasks is considered blocking.

In the case of multiple processor environments, a task may also have to wait for a task running on a remote processor to release a shared resource, and the concept of waiting needs to be generalized to include *remote* blocking. When a job has to wait for the execution of a task of *any* priority assigned to another processor, it is said to experience remote blocking. The justification is as follows. If there were no resource sharing between the tasks on different processors, a task cannot be blocked by *any* task on another processor. Thus, in multiple processor systems, blocking can be caused by any task of higher, equal or lower priority on another processor.

The concept of "remote blocking" as defined above can be confusing at first sight. In a priority-based environment, why should the time that a task on one processor waits for a *higher* priority task on another processor be

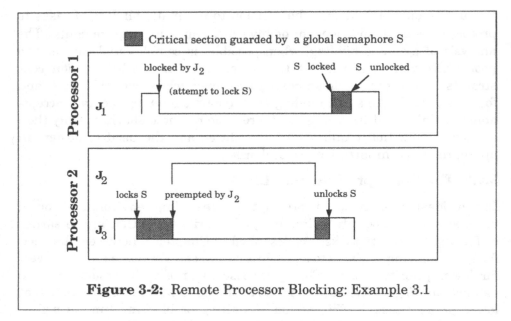

Figure 3-2: Remote Processor Blocking: Example 3.1

considered blocking? The reason is that with independent tasks with no resource-sharing, this waiting would not have taken place. From an analytical perspective, when static binding of tasks to processors is used and there is no resource-sharing, the schedulability of each processor in the system can be checked independent of the others. But once resource-sharing is introduced, if a task is forced to wait for a task of *any* priority on another processor, the schedulability test on a processor must include this additional waiting time which does not exist in the absence of shared resources. As a result, it is the concept of remote blocking and not priority inversion that is directly applicable across processors in a multiple processor environment.

One of our basic objectives is to minimize the *remote* blocking time in the design of multiple processor synchronization protocols. Minimized blocking directly translates to additional schedulable utilization on each processor as we shall see in Section 2.6.

Example 3.1: Consider normal prioritized execution without priority inheritance in effect. Suppose that task τ_1 is bound to processor $\wp_1$, and that tasks τ_2 and τ_3 are bound to processor $\wp_2$. As shown in Figure 3-2, suppose that J_1 is executing on

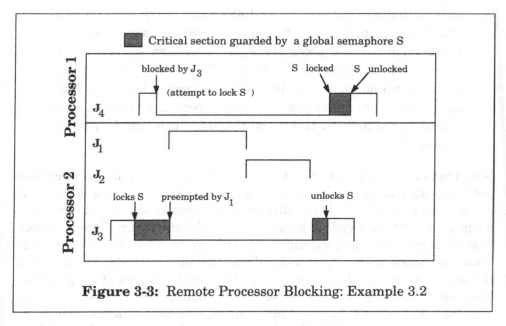

Figure 3-3: Remote Processor Blocking: Example 3.2

processor $\wp_1$ and wants to lock semaphore S. But S is currently locked by job J_3 executing on processor $\wp_2$. Job J_1 is now said to encounter remote blocking. If there were no shared data, J_1 would not be blocked and will continue to execute. One might again expect that J_1 will be blocked only for the duration of J_3's execution of its critical section. However, if J_2 now preempts J_3 on processor $\wp_2$, J_1 will be blocked until J_2 completes (or blocks) to allow J_3 to resume and release S. The blocking time of J_1 will continue until J_2 and any other intermediate priority jobs on $\wp_2$ complete execution or suspend themselves.

With priority inheritance in effect in Example 3.1, J_3 will inherit J_1's higher priority and complete its critical section without being preempted by J_2 or other intermediate priority jobs. Once J_3 releases S, J_1 would be able to resume. Thus, priority inheritance seems to solve this particular situation of unbounded blocking. However, let us now consider the following example illustrated in Figure 3-3.

Example 3.2: Suppose that tasks τ_1, τ_2 and τ_3 are bound to processor $\wp_2$ and that task τ_4 is bound to processor $\wp_1$. Job J_4

is executing on processor $\wp_1$ and attempts to lock semaphore S. But S is currently locked by job J_3 executing on processor $\wp_2$. However, if J_1 now preempts J_3 on processor $\wp_2$, J_4 will be blocked until J_1 completes (or blocks). Thus, the blocking time of J_4 will continue until arriving higher priority jobs on $\wp_2$ (such as J_1 and J_2) complete execution or suspend themselves. Since τ_1 and τ_2 are periodic tasks, the blocking duration of J_4 can be arbitrarily long.

Note that in Example 3.2, even the imposition of priority inheritance does *not* force any changes in the event sequence, and the blocking duration of J_4 remains unchanged. It can also be easily seen that a direct use of the uniprocessor priority ceiling protocol does not induce any changes either. The blocking duration of J_4, unfortunately, can be a function of the entire execution times of jobs J_1 and J_2. This example illustrates the fact that the nature of remote blocking is very different from that of uniprocessor blocking. Blocking, as mentioned earlier, can be considered to be the duration that a task has to wait compared to the situation where no semaphores are present. In the absence of any data-sharing, J_4 would not have to wait at all, and its blocking duration now becomes a function of execution times of tasks on other processors.

The situation in Example 3.2 cannot be improved directly with either priority inheritance or the priority ceiling protocol. This gives rise to the need for new synchronization protocols for multiple processor systems. Shared memory multiprocessors may allow atomic operations such as test-and-set on shared memory to implement global synchronization, whereas message-passing must be resorted to in distributed systems. This dichotomy leads us to develop two protocols, one for multiprocessors and another for distributed systems.

Our goal is to design synchronization protocols that bound the remote blocking duration of a job as a function of the duration of critical sections of other jobs and *not* as a function of the duration of executing non-critical section code. In other words, we forbid situations where a job J has to be blocked on one processor while another job executes on another processor outside a critical section preventing J from being unblocked. For instance, in Example 3.2, jobs J_1 and J_2 should not be allowed to execute outside their critical sections while job J_4 is blocked waiting for them to complete.

The motivation behind this goal is the observation that a critical section is very small relative to the task execution time.

Another fundamental goal of our synchronization protocols is that whenever possible, we would let a lower priority job wait for a higher priority job. For example, if two jobs J_H and J_L are waiting for the release of a shared resource, the higher priority job J_H will be allowed to access the resource first even if J_L has been waiting for a longer duration. Such situations arise, for instance, when these two jobs are executing on two different processors and need a shared resource currently locked by a job on a third processor. Given a certain blocking duration B for a job J and a period T for the corresponding task τ, the ratio B/T is a measure of schedulability loss due to blocking. Under the rate-monotonic scheduling algorithm, a lower priority job has a longer period and hence less schedulability loss results if we let the lower priority job wait.[15] This objective is also reflected in our prioritized queues on the semaphores accessed by real-time tasks.

In summary, our approach differs inherently from global synchronization techniques like those proposed by Gait [Gait 87] where tasks access semaphores on a FIFO basis. Our primary objective is to minimize the schedulability loss due to both local blocking and remote blocking and is represented as two sub-goals. The first goal is that the worst-case blocking duration B of a job should be a function of critical section durations only. The second goal is to minimize the impact of B whenever possible by letting a lower priority job rather than a higher priority job experience blocking. A major result of the second goal is our priority queue for jobs blocked on semaphores. Apart from this ordering, these two goals conflict to a small degree in that the first goal may sometimes require that a higher priority job has to wait for a lower priority job.

---

[15]As discussed in Chapter 1, tasks with shorter periods need not necessarily have higher semantic importance to the mission. This need for combining semantic importance with the priority assignment policy can be achieved using *period transformation* [Sha 86], a technique that maintains the optimality of the rate-monotonic scheduling algorithm.

3.2.4. Assumptions and Notation

The following assumptions and notation are used throughout this chapter. We assume that prioritized preemptive scheduling and static binding of tasks to processors are used. In particular, we assume that tasks are assigned priorities according to the rate-monotonic scheduling algorithm. We also assume that at any given instant, the highest priority task ready to run on a given processor is executing on each of the processors.

We assume that binary semaphores are used for task synchronization. A semaphore that is accessed by tasks allocated to different processors is referred to as a *global semaphore*, and a critical section guarded by a global semaphore is referred to as a *global critical section* (gcs). Similarly, a semaphore that is accessed by tasks allocated to a single processor is called a *local semaphore*, and a critical section guarded by a local semaphore is referred to as a *local critical section* (lcs). Note that if there are no global semaphores in the system, the multiple processor synchronization problem decomposes into multiple uniprocessor problems and the uniprocessor priority ceiling protocol (or the semaphore control protocol) can be used very effectively on each processor.

In this chapter, we assume that global critical sections do not make any nested access to local semaphores, and that local critical sections do not make any nested access to global semaphores. As we shall see, global semaphore accesses can potentially lead to high increases in blocking durations. Hence, we assume that efforts have been made to allocate tasks accessing the same semaphore to the same processor as far as possible. We describe a possible approach to task allocation in Section 3.4.

3.2.5. Global and Local Priority Ceilings

The notion of the priority ceiling of a semaphore needs to be extended to global semaphores. We begin with a Lemma on a property of the priority ceiling of semaphores in uniprocessors.

> **Lemma 3-1:** The priority ceiling of a semaphore S represents the maximum priority at which an outermost critical section

guarded by this semaphore can execute.[16]

Proof: Consider an outermost critical section z of τ which is guarded by a semaphore S at a priority ceiling P. According to Lemma 2-9, the priority ceiling protocol prevents transitive blocking. Hence, z can execute at a higher priority only if τ is inside z, and another task τ_h with higher priority than τ is blocked by z. As a result, z would inherit τ_h's priority. However, by the definition of the protocol, for τ_h to be blocked by z, τ_h must have a priority lower than or equal to the priority ceiling of S. The Lemma follows.

In order to extend the priority ceiling protocol to multiple processor systems, this property of the priority ceiling of a semaphore is maintained.

<u>Notation:</u> The notation P_i is used interchangeably with $p(J_i)$, the priority of job J_i.

<u>Notation:</u> The assigned priority of the highest priority task on processor $\wp_i$ is denoted by P_{H_i}.

<u>Notation:</u> The assigned priority of the highest priority task in the system is denoted by P_H, i.e. $P_H = \max(P_{H_i})$.

Under the uniprocessor priority ceiling protocol, no critical section will be executed at a priority higher than the highest priority of any task in the system. Hence, the priority ceiling of any local semaphore will be less than or equal to P_H. However, on multiple processor systems, global critical sections may need to execute at a priority higher than the highest assigned priority to tasks. The following theorem shows that this must be

---

[16]This property applies only to outermost critical sections and not to inner critical sections. For example, consider a nested critical section z of a task τ_3, the outer guarded by S_1 and the inner by S_2. If task τ_1 can lock S_1, and τ_2 can lock S_2, the priority ceilings of S_1 and S_2 are P_1 and P_2 respectively. If τ_3 locks S_1, and then τ_1 needs S_1, τ_3 will inherit τ_1's priority until it exits z. This also implies that the inner critical section guarded by S_2 executes at priority P_1, which is greater than its priority ceiling. Similarly, an inner critical section can be guarded by a semaphore with a higher priority ceiling than that of a semaphore guarding its outermost critical section. In this case, the inner critical section alone can execute at a higher priority than the outermost critical section. This priority inheritance is attributed only to the inner critical section and *not* to the outermost critical section.

the case in order to obtain task blocking durations that are functions of critical section durations only.

Theorem 3-2: The remote blocking time of a job blocked on a global critical section will be a function of critical sections if and only if the global critical section cannot be preempted by jobs that are executing outside critical sections.

Proof: First, if global critical sections cannot be preempted by non-critical section code, then the waiting time for entering a gcs can only be a function of critical sections. Second, if a gcs on a processor can be preempted by the non-critical section code of J, then a job on another processor blocked by this gcs will wait for the execution time of J.

Recall that our goal was to render the worst-case blocking duration of a job as a function of critical section durations only. Hence, by Theorem 3-2, when a job is waiting for a global semaphore S_G, we should allow the gcs on $\wp_i$ that will release S_G to execute at a priority higher than P_{H_i}. It is convenient to assume, without loss of generality, that this value of priority is higher than the assigned priorities of *all* tasks in the system, namely P_H.

Since the priority ceiling of a semaphore S is the highest priority that an (outermost) critical section guarded by S can execute, a global semaphore has to be assigned a priority ceiling which is higher than the highest assigned priority of all tasks in the system. Such a constraint does not apply to local semaphores. Thus, we need to define two types of priority ceilings, one for local semaphores and one for global semaphores.

Definition: The priority ceiling of a local semaphore S is defined to be the priority of the highest priority task that may lock the semaphore S.

Definition: Let the priority of the highest priority task that accesses a semaphore S_i be denoted by PS_i. Then, the priority ceiling of a global semaphore S_j is defined such that

- The priority ceiling of S_j is higher than P_H.

- If S_i and S_j are global semaphores and $PS_i > PS_j$, then the priority ceiling of S_i is greater than the priority ceiling of S_j.

This set of conditions can be met, for example, as follows. Define the *base priority ceiling* P_G of a global semaphore as a fixed priority that is higher than P_H[17]. Then, the priority ceiling of a global semaphore can be the sum of the priority of the highest priority task accessing the semaphore and the base priority ceiling P_G. This assignment maintains the ordering of the priority ceilings and ensures that the priority ceilings of all global semaphores are higher than P_H.

We shall further illustrate this terminology in Sections 3.3 and 3.5.

3.3 THE DISTRIBUTED PRIORITY CEILING PROTOCOL

In this section, we develop a priority ceiling protocol suitable for synchronizing tasks executing on distributed systems. In other words, the protocols relies only on message-passing between processors and uses a remote procedure call model.

3.3.1. Synchronization Processors

Jobs are first bound to processors. While a job J always executes local critical sections and non-critical-section code on its host processor, its global critical sections are bound to and executed on a processor which can be other than J's host processor. All global critical sections associated with the same global semaphore S must be bound to the same processor. This means that each global semaphore S_G is bound to a processor $\wp_G$, and all jobs that need to lock S_G need to execute the corresponding gcs on $\wp_G$. Thus, all gcs's will be executed on specially marked processors to isolate the blocking durations caused by global semaphores. This scheme helps in distributed systems where global shared resources can be handled in centralized locations and services offered via message-based remote procedure calls between processors. Server tasks can replace specialized global critical section code.

Processors which execute global critical sections are called *synchronization processors*. Clearly, there can be multiple synchronization processors in a system. The only requirement is that all gcs's guarded by the same global semaphore must be bound to the same synchronization processor. The processor where all the gcs's of a global semaphore S_G is executed is referred to as S_G's synchronization processor.

---

[17]An example of P_G can be P_H+1 if higher values mean higher priorities.

3.3.2. Normal Execution Priority of a GCS

Theorem 3-2 only requires that a gcs guarded by a global semaphore S_G be executed at higher priority than tasks executing outside critical sections when a remote task is blocked by S_G. However, for ease of implementation, we always execute a gcs at higher priority than all tasks outside critical sections. The assigned priority at which a gcs executes is defined as follows:

<u>Definition</u>: The assigned priority at which a global critical section z_j of job J_j executes is defined such that

- The priority is higher than P_H.
- If the priority of J_i is greater than the priority of J_j, then the priority assigned to gcs z_i is greater than the priority assigned to gcs z_j.

This set of conditions can also be met as follows. A global critical section z_i can be assigned a priority equal to the sum of the base priority ceiling P_G and P_i, the priority of J_i.

3.3.3. Terminology Illustration

We illustrate the terminology developed so far using the following example. Figure 3-4 depicts the binding of tasks and semaphores to processors.

> **Example 3.3:** Suppose that there are three processors $\wp_1$, $\wp_2$ and $\wp_3$ in the system. The application consists of 4 tasks and 4 semaphores. Let tasks τ_1 and τ_3 be bound to processor $\wp_1$, and tasks τ_2 and τ_4 be bound to processor $\wp_2$. The jobs J_1, J_2, J_3 and J_4 have the following sequence of steps:
>
> $$J_1 = \{ \cdots, \mathbf{P}(S_3), \cdots, \mathbf{V}(S_3), \cdots, \mathbf{P}(S_1), \cdots, \mathbf{V}(S_1), \cdots \}$$
> $$J_2 = \{ \cdots, \mathbf{P}(S_3), \cdots, \mathbf{V}(S_3), \cdots, \mathbf{P}(S_2), \cdots, \mathbf{V}(S_2), \cdots \}$$
> $$J_3 = \{ \cdots, \mathbf{P}(S_1), \cdots, \mathbf{V}(S_1), \cdots, \mathbf{P}(S_4), \cdots, \mathbf{V}(S_4), \cdots \}$$
> $$J_4 = \{ \cdots, \mathbf{P}(S_2), \cdots, \mathbf{V}(S_2), \cdots, \mathbf{P}(S_4), \cdots, \mathbf{V}(S_4), \cdots \}$$
>
> The semaphores S_1 and S_2 can be bound to $\wp_1$ and $\wp_2$ respectively, since they are being accessed only by tasks bound to their corresponding processors. Hence, S_1 (S_2) is a local semaphore on $\wp_1$ $(\wp_2)$. A critical section guarded by S_1 (S_2) is considered an

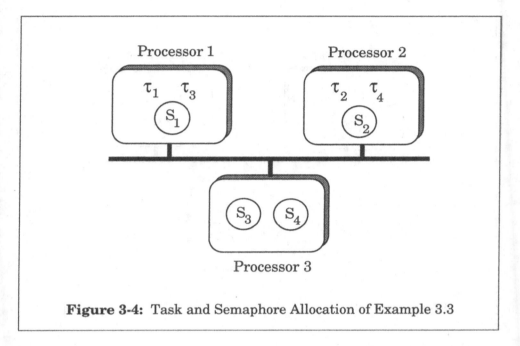

Figure 3-4: Task and Semaphore Allocation of Example 3.3

'lcs' on $\wp_1$ ($\wp_2$). Since semaphores S_3 and S_4 will be locked by tasks bound to different processors, they are called global semaphores, and critical sections guarded by either of them is called a 'gcs'. We assume that every gcs is executed on processor $\wp_3$ which acts as the synchronization processor for S_3 and S_4. Synchronization processor $\wp_3$ could still run other tasks, say task τ_5, if the latter is bound to it. In contrast, processors $\wp_1$ and $\wp_2$ execute *only* non-gcs code.

3.3.4. Implementation Considerations

A job attempting to access a global semaphore on a synchronization processor can be considered to "migrate" to the synchronization processor for the execution of its global critical section (as a remote procedure call). In reality, tasks can be statically bound to their host processors and a thread of execution for each (outermost) global critical section can be created on the synchronization processor. The thread is assigned the priority of its remote caller. Once the job exits the global critical section, it can be considered to migrate back to its host processor. In other words, control is returned to the calling thread. This allows us to refer to the

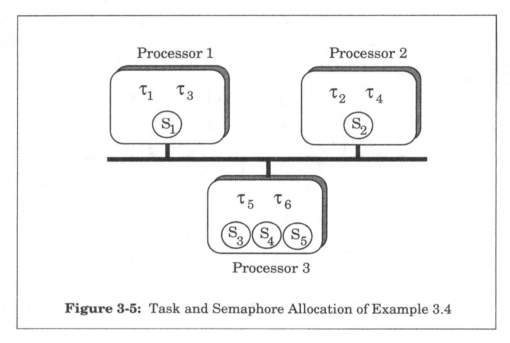

Figure 3-5: Task and Semaphore Allocation of Example 3.4

thread of execution within a critical section by the job J on whose behalf the critical section is being executed. From an implementation point of view, the actual gcs execution can be carried out by an agent task J' of J on the synchronization processor. Also, when a job is executing a gcs on a synchronization processor, its host processor is free and can be used to execute a lower priority job not in a gcs.

3.3.5. Illustration of the Distributed Protocol

We illustrate the concepts of global priority ceiling and normal execution priority of a gcs in the following example. The binding of tasks and semaphores to processors is illustrated in Figure 3-5.

Example 3.4: Consider a multiple processor system with 3 processors $\wp_1$, $\wp_2$ and $\wp_3$. The application is comprised of 6 tasks and 5 semaphores. The task pairs $\{\tau_1, \tau_3\}$, $\{\tau_2, \tau_4\}$ and $\{\tau_5, \tau_6\}$ are bound to processors $\wp_1$, $\wp_2$ and $\wp_3$ respectively. Jobs J_1, J_2, J_3, J_4, J_5 and J_6 execute the following sequence of steps:

$$J_1 = \{\cdots, \mathbf{P}(S_3), \cdots, \mathbf{V}(S_3), \cdots, \mathbf{P}(S_1), \cdots, \mathbf{V}(S_1), \cdots\}$$
$$J_2 = \{\cdots, \mathbf{P}(S_3), \cdots, \mathbf{V}(S_3), \cdots, \mathbf{P}(S_2), \cdots, \mathbf{V}(S_2), \cdots\}$$
$$J_3 = \{\cdots, \mathbf{P}(S_1), \cdots, \mathbf{V}(S_1), \cdots, \mathbf{P}(S_4), \cdots, \mathbf{V}(S_4), \cdots\}$$

Priority Ceilings of Semaphores	
Semaphore	Priority Ceiling
S_1 (local)	$p(J_1)$
S_2 (local)	$p(J_2)$
S_3 (global)	$P_G + p(J_1)$
S_4 (global)	$P_G + p(J_3)$
S_5 (local)	$p(J_5)$

Table 3-1: The Priority Ceilings of Semaphores in Example 3.4

$J_4 = \{\cdots, P(S_2), \cdots, V(S_2), \cdots, P(S_4), \cdots, V(S_4), \cdots\}$
$J_5 = \{\cdots, P(S_3), \cdots, V(S_3), \cdots, P(S_5), \cdots, V(S_5), \cdots\}$
$J_6 = \{\cdots, P(S_4), \cdots, V(S_4), \cdots, P(S_5), \cdots, V(S_5), \cdots\}$

That is, we add semaphore S_5 and tasks τ_5 and τ_6 to the task set of Example 3.3. As before, local semaphore S_1 (S_2) is bound to $\wp_1$ ($\wp_2$), and the global semaphores S_3 and S_4 are bound to $\wp_3$. The new semaphore S_5 is local to $\wp_3$.

Define the base priority ceiling P_G to be $p(J_1) + 1$. Recall that $p(J_i) > p(J_{i+1})$. Then, the priority ceiling of each semaphore, and the normal execution priority of each critical section thread are listed in Tables 3-1 and 3-2 respectively.

An agent task J' of a job J on a synchronization processor executes the gcs on behalf of J. Since J' only executes gcs's on J's behalf, J' can be assigned the normal gcs execution priority of J as listed in Table 3-2.

3.3.6. The Definition of the Distributed Priority Ceiling Protocol

We now define the distributed priority ceiling protocol that is used in each of the system processors..

- The priority ceilings of global semaphores are defined as described.

- Each global critical section on its synchronization processor normally executes at its assigned priority.

Normal Execution Priorities of Critical Sections		
Job	Critical Section Guarded by	Execution Priority
J_1	S_1 S_3	$p(J_1)$ $P_G + p(J_1)$
J_2	S_2 S_3	$p(J_2)$ $P_G + p(J_2)$
J_3	S_1 S_4	$p(J_3)$ $P_G + p(J_3)$
J_4	S_2 S_4	$p(J_4)$ $P_G + p(J_4)$
J_5	S_3 S_5	$P_G + p(J_5)$ $p(J_5)$
J_6	S_4 S_5	$P_G + p(J_6)$ $p(J_6)$

Table 3-2: The Normal Execution Priorities of Critical Sections in Example 3.4

- Each processor runs the priority ceiling protocol on the global critical sections (considering each thread of execution for executing a global critical section as a "job"), the set of application tasks (if any), and the set of global and local semaphores bound to the processor.

Note that by the definition of the protocol, gcs execution on any of the processors will preempt an application task.

Remark: An application job J bound to a synchronization processor $\wp_G$ can be preempted by a lower priority job J_i bound to another processor if J_i executes a gcs on $\wp_G$. Such priority inversion can be avoided by allocating only the lowest priority jobs to synchronization processors.

Suppose that we have m synchronization processors. We disallow locks on global semaphores to be held across processor boundaries, i.e. a gcs executing on its synchronization processor $\wp_G$ cannot request a *nested* lock on a global semaphore allocated to a different processor. The primary reason behind this constraint is that such locking leads to excessive blocking durations with a cross-coupling between the processors. For example, consider a critical section on $\wp_{G_1}$ attempting to lock a semaphore S on $\wp_{G_2}$. Tasks on $\wp_{G_1}$ can now encounter remote blocking from global critical sections on $\wp_{G_2}$ and vice-versa. The net blocking effect is similar to allocating global critical sections executing on both processors to the same processor and may even be worse. We shall, however, defer the discussion of task allocation to Section 3.4.

We illustrate the distributed priority ceiling protocol using the following example.

Example 3.5: Consider the 3-processor system with the 6-task set and the 5 semaphores defined in Example 3.4. The priority ceilings of these semaphores and the normal execution priorities of the gcs's in the system are listed in Tables 3-1 and 3-2 respectively.

Consider the following sequence of events illustrated in Figure 3-6.

- At time t_0, job J_3 arrives on processor 1 and begins execution. Similarly, job J_6 begins execution on processor 3. Processor 2 is idle.

- At time t_1, J_1 arrives on processor 1 and preempts J_3. Job J_4 begins execution on processor 2. Job J_6 locks the global semaphore S_4 on processor 3, and begins execution of the gcs at its normal execution priority of $P_G+p(J_6)$.

- At time t_2, J_1 needs global semaphore S_3, and invokes a remote procedure call to S_3's synchronization processor 3. Its local agent task on processor 3 J_1' has the priority of $P_G+p(J_1)$ which is greater than the global priority ceiling of locked global semaphore (on processor 3) S_4, $P_G+p(J_3)$. As a result, J_1' is allowed to lock S_3, and preempts the gcs execution of J_6 on processor 3. Since processor 1 is idle, J_3 resumes execution. Job J_4 locks the local semaphore S_2 on processor 2 in which no semaphores have been locked by other jobs. Meanwhile, J_5 becomes ready for execution on processor 3, but is unable to preempt J_1'.

- At time t_3, J_1' exits its gcs guarded by S_3 on processor 3, and

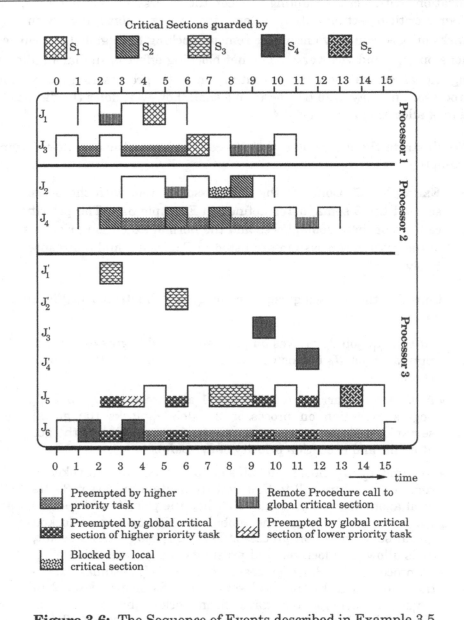

Figure 3-6: The Sequence of Events described in Example 3.5

J_1 resumes execution on processor 1 preempting job J_3. Job J_2 arrives on processor 2, and having higher priority, immediately preempts J_4. Job J_6 resumes its gcs execution on processor 3.

- At time t_4, J_1 locks the local semaphore S_1 on processor 1. Job J_2 continues non-critical section execution on processor 2. On processor 3, J_6 exits its gcs guarded by S_4 and resumes its assigned priority of $p(J_6)$. Immediately, it is preempted by J_5.

- At time t_5, J_1 releases the local semaphore S_1 and continues execution outside its critical section. On processor 2, J_2 issues a request to lock global semaphore S_3. Its agent task J'_2 has an assigned priority of $P_G+p(J_2)$ and immediately preempts J_5. Job J_4 resumes its critical section execution on processor 2.

- At time t_6, J_1 completes execution. Job J_3 resumes and then locks local semaphore S_1. On processor 3, J'_2 exits its gcs. Job J_2 regains control and preempts J_4 on processor 2. Job J_5 resumes on processor 3.

- At time t_7, J_3 releases the local semaphore S_1 and continues execution on processor 1. On processor 2, J_2 attempts to lock S_2. However, the run-time system on processor 2 finds that $p(J_2)$ is not greater than $c(S_2) = p(J_2)$ and blocks J_2. Job J_4 inherits J_2's priority and resumes execution of its critical section on processor 2. Job J_5 locks global semaphore S_3 on processor 3.

- At time t_8, J_3 needs to lock global semaphore S_4. However, the priority of its agent task J'_3 on processor 3, $P_G+p(J_3) < c(S_3) = P_G+p(J_1)$. Hence, J'_3 is blocked, and J_5 resumes its gcs execution at the inherited priority of $P_G+p(J_3)$. Since there are no ready jobs, processor 1 becomes idle. On processor 2, J_4 releases S_2 and resumes its normal priority allowing J_2 to preempt it and lock S_2.

- At time t_9, processor 1 continues to be idle. Job J_2 releases S_2 on processor 2 and continues to execute. On processor 3, J_5 releases S_3 and resumes its low assigned priority. Immediately, J'_3 preempts J_5 and locks S_4.

- At time t_{10}, J'_3 exits its gcs on processor 3 by releasing S_4. Hence, J_3 resumes execution on processor 1. On processor 2,

J_2 completes and J_4 resumes execution. Job J_5 resumes execution on processor 3.

- At time t_{11}, J_3 completes on processor 1 which turns idle. Job J_4 needs to lock global semaphore S_4, and its agent task J'_4 on processor 2 preempts J_5 with its higher priority of $P_G + \rho(J_4)$.

- At time t_{12}, J'_4 releases S_4 and J_4 resumes execution on processor 2. Job J_5 resumes on processor 3.

- At time t_{13}, J_4 completes execution on processor 2 which turns idle. On processor 3, J_5 locks S_5.

- At time t_{14}, J_5 releases S_5 and completes at time t_{15}. Finally, J_6 is free to resume, lock and release S_5 and later complete.

The above example illustrates the following features of the protocol:

- A gcs always preempts the execution of non-gcs code. This happens at t_5 on processor 3.

- The execution of one gcs can preempt the execution of another gcs guarded by S_G if the priority of the former thread is greater than the priority ceiling of S_G. This happens at t_2 on processor 3. If this condition is not satisfied, an unlocked global semaphore will not be allowed to be locked. This happens at t_8 on processor 3.

- The local priority ceiling condition is used for local semaphore requests. An example occurs at t_7 on processor 2.

- An idle processor can be used by a lower priority ready job. This happens at t_2 on processor 1, and at t_5 on processor 2.

- Application tasks can soak up idle time on a synchronization processor. For example, jobs J_5 and J_6 use the idle time available on processor 3.

3.3.7. Effects of Deferred Execution

Liu and Layland's original schedulability analysis of the rate-monotonic scheduling algorithm [Liu 73] assumes that a periodic task arrives at periodic intervals and executes from initiation to completion without any suspensions. However, in the current scenario, a job can suspend itself waiting for a global semaphore to be released and this waiting duration can vary depending upon whether a global semaphore is locked and upon the requests from other jobs. As a result, a high priority job may be

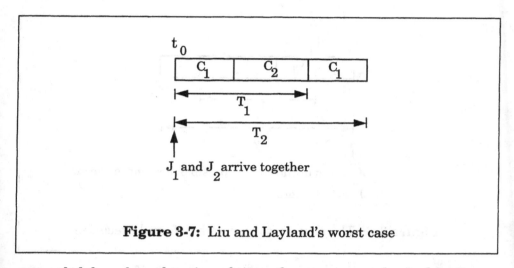

Figure 3-7: Liu and Layland's worst case

suspended for a long duration of time, then resume and complete its execution to *just* meet its deadline at the end of the period. The next job instantiation arrives immediately and may now run to completion since all requests happen to be satisfied. Thus, a high priority job J_H can delay itself and then inflict "back-to-back hits" on a lower priority job J_i that is initiated at the instant of J_H's resumption. For instance, in the Liu and Layland analysis, the worst case occurs when $T_i/T_1 < 2$ and the lower priority job J_i is preempted at most twice. This is shown in Figure 3-7. However, in our context, the sequence shown in Figure 3-8 can occur. Task τ_1 arrives at t_1-T_1 and at t_1, while τ_2 arrives at $t_0 = t_1-C_1$. However, only the first instance of τ_1 defers its execution and begins execution at time t_0. As a result, even if $T_i/T_1 < 2$, job J_i can be preempted 3 times before its deadline. This additional preemption leads to a scheduling penalty and is identical to that caused by the deferred server algorithm used to service aperiodic tasks [Strosnider 88].

The scheduling penalty of deferred execution can be fairly large and can cause the schedulable utilization of different processors to be unacceptably low. Fortunately, this scheduling penalty can be eliminated completely by using a technique called the *Period Enforcer* [Rajkumar 91]. In this context, the primary idea behind this technique is to ensure that whenever a task τ_i tries to enter a gcs on a different processor and can therefore suspend, the instants at which its jobs resume execution must not be

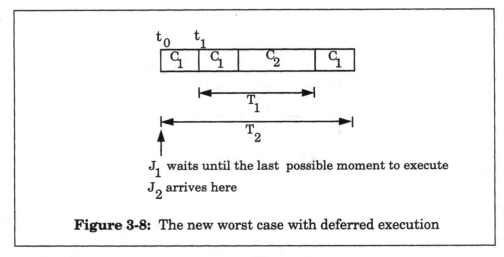

Figure 3-8: The new worst case with deferred execution

separated by less than its period T_i.[18] For example, if one instance of a task resumes execution at time t_0, its next instance will not be allowed to resume execution before time $t_0 + T_i$. Similarly, the instants at which the remote procedure call requests are handled at the synchronization processor must not be separated by less than its period T_i.

In our subsequent discussions of the distributed priority ceiling protocol, we shall assume that the period enforcer technique is being used.

3.3.8. Properties of the Distributed Priority Ceiling Protocol

The distributed priority ceiling protocol prevents deadlocks and bounds the blocking duration of each task as a function of the critical section durations of other tasks. We shall prove these properties in this section.

Theorem 3-3: Under the distributed priority ceiling protocol, deadlocks are avoided.

Proof: First, by assumption, a job cannot deadlock with itself. Hence, a job can only deadlock with some other job. Also, by assumption, global critical sections do not access local semaphores and vice-versa. Hence, access to global and local semaphores cannot occur within the same critical section. Since every global and local semaphore is accessed only by a single processor, dead-

---

[18]It is possible that two successive jobs can be separated by less than a period but then other conditions related to priority need to be satisfied. A more detailed discussion can be found in [Rajkumar 91].

locks cannot occur across processor boundaries. The priority ceiling protocol which is used on each processor avoids deadlocks within a processor. The Theorem follows.

We now compute the maximum blocking duration that each job can encounter.

<u>Notation</u>: Let n_i^G represent the number of (outermost) global critical sections that a job J_i executes before its completion. Again, a nested critical section like $\{P(S_1) \cdots P(S_2) \cdots V(S_2), \cdots, V(S_1)\}$ is considered to be a single critical section.

<u>Remark</u>: Each time a job J needs to enter a gcs, it suspends on its host processor $\wp$. During this suspension, lower priority jobs on $\wp$ can execute and lock a local semaphore. This locking can contribute to additional blocking to J on the host processor, when it resumes (after the execution of its gcs at the synchronization processor). The next theorem provides a bound for this blocking duration at the local processor.

Theorem 3-4: A job J_i bound to a processor $\wp$ can be blocked for the durations of at most n_i^G+1 local critical sections of lower priority jobs bound to $\wp$.

Proof: Job J can be considered to be suspending itself when it attempts to enter a global critical section which will be executed on $\wp_G$. The Theorem follows from Corollary 2-13.

<u>Notation</u>: Let $n_{i,j}^G$ represent the number of (outermost) global critical sections on $\wp_j$ that a job J_i enters before its completion. We have $\sum_j n_{i,j}^G = n_i^G$.

<u>Notation</u>: Let the sum of the durations that a job J_i spends within global critical sections, when executing alone on the synchronization processor(s), be represented by CS_i.

<u>Notation</u>: Let the sum of the durations that a job J_i spends within global critical sections on processor $\wp_j$, when executing alone on the processor, be represented by $CS_{i,j}$. Thus, we have $\sum_j CS_{i,j} = CS_i$.

<u>Remark</u>: When a job J attempts to enter a gcs z, it can be blocked by a locked global semaphore S executing on the synchronization processor if the assigned priority of z is not greater than the global priority ceiling of S. The next two theorems present an upper bound on this blocking duration.

Theorem 3-5: A job J can wait for a duration of at most $(CS_{i,k} \times \lceil T/T_i \rceil)$ of a higher priority job J_i on a synchronization processor $\wp_k$ during its period T.

Proof: During the interval T, J_i can execute for a maximum duration of $(CS_{i,k} \times \lceil T/T_i \rceil)$ in the synchronization processor $\wp_k$. The Theorem follows.

Theorem 3-6: For every (outermost) gcs that J_i enters on a synchronization processor $\wp_k$, J_i can be blocked for the duration of at most the duration of one global critical section of all lower priority jobs on $\wp_k$.

Proof: The Theorem follows directly from Theorem 2-12 and the fact that each global critical section duration can be considered to be a job.

3.3.9. Schedulability Analysis

Theorems 3-4, 3-5 and 3-6 lead to sufficient conditions for a job J bound to a processor $\wp$ to meet its deadline.

For the sake of convenience, we repeat Theorem 2-16 below.

Theorem 3-7: A set of n periodic tasks using the priority ceiling protocol can be scheduled by the rate-monotonic algorithm if the following conditions are satisfied:

$$\forall\, i,\ 1 \le i \le n,\quad \frac{C_1}{T_1} + \frac{C_2}{T_2} + \cdots + \frac{C_i}{T_i} + \frac{B_i}{T_i} \le i(2^{1/i} - 1)$$

We test the above set of inequalities for each processor $\wp$ where n is the number of tasks bound to $\wp$, and C_k and T_k are the computation time and the period, respectively, of task τ_k bound to $\wp$. The term B_i is the maximum duration that a job J bound to $\wp$ can be blocked from initiation to completion. Since we use the priority ceiling protocol on each of the processors, Theorem 3-7 applies. Once B_i has been computed for all i, Theorem 3-7 can then be used to determine the schedulability of each processor.

When there are multiple synchronization processors, their utilization will be generally low and application tasks can easily be added to these synchronization processors. Tasks bound to synchronization processors would encounter local blocking from these global critical sections as well.

Suppose that J_i is bound to a processor $\wp$. Then B_i is the sum of

1. Duration of $n_i^G + 1$ local critical sections on $\wp$ that can block J_i. Under the priority ceiling protocol, a critical section z of a lower priority job guarded by a semaphore S can block J_i only if J_i's priority is not strictly higher than the priority ceiling of S. Let Z_L be the set of local critical sections that can block J_i. Hence, by Theorem 3-4, the upper bound of this type of blocking is n_i^G times the duration of the longest element in Z_L.

2. A maximum duration of n_i^G global critical sections of lower priority jobs on remote synchronization processors accessed by J_i. By Theorem 3-6, whenever J_i tries to lock a global semaphore on a remote synchronization processor, its remote agent acts as a "job" and can be blocked for the duration of one gcs of a lower priority task on that processor. A global critical section z of a lower priority job can block J_i only if the assigned priority of J_i's gcs is not strictly higher than the priority ceiling of the semaphore guarding z.

3. Duration of global critical sections of higher priority jobs bound to synchronization processors other than $\wp$ which would also be accessed by J_i. By Theorem 3-5, on each synchronization processor $\wp_k$ other than $\wp$ that J_i accesses, the gcs's of a higher priority task τ_m can block J_i for a duration of at most $(CS_{m,k} \times \lceil T_i/T_m \rceil)$. The sum of these blocking durations for all J_k yields the worst-case blocking for this type of blocking.

4. Duration of gcs's of lower priority tasks bound to J_i's host processor. If a task is bound to a synchronization processor, its execution can be preempted by every gcs execution on this processor. The blocking time of task τ_i due to global critical sections is

$$B_i = \sum_{j \in R} CS_j \times \lceil T_i/T_j \rceil$$

where R is the set of lower priority tasks that may use a global semaphore bound to this processor.

The sum of the above four quantities yields B_i which, in turn, can be used in Theorem 3-7 to determine whether the task set for the current task allocation to $\wp$ is schedulable. Clearly, global critical sections must be short relative to task periods in order to maintain a high level of schedulability.

Remark: It must be noted that the above computation of B_i yields a pessimistic bound and can be reduced by considering the exact time of references to global semaphores relative to a task period.

Remark: On a synchronization processor, global critical sections always execute at a priority greater than P_H and use the priority ceiling protocol. That is, in order for a gcs to lock a global semaphore and begin execution, it must have a normal priority greater than the highest priority ceiling of locked global semaphores on the processor. That is, once a gcs z guarded by a semaphore S_G begins execution, only another gcs with an assigned priority greater than the global priority ceiling of S_G can preempt z. The net result is that a gcs guarded by a semaphore S_G always executes at an effective priority equal to the priority ceiling of S_G. In other words, the priority ceiling protocol used by the gcs's is identical to the ceiling semaphore protocol described in Section 2.6. An implementation can exploit this property by assigning a gcs z guarded by a global semaphore S a priority equal to the priority ceiling of S.

3.3.10. A Schedulability Analysis Example

In this section, we illustrate the schedulability analysis described in the previous section with the task set used in Examples 3.4 and 3.5. This walk-through example also serves to illustrate the fact that the blocking factor determined is an upper bound and can be pessimistic. We therefore use additional information about the task set and exploit properties of the priority ceiling protocol when possible to reduce the worst-case blocking duration of a task.

The periods and computation times within and outside critical sections for each task are listed in Table 3-3 in the order of processor bindings. These computation times correspond to the illustration in Figure 3-6. Since τ_6's computation profile is not complete, we assume that τ_6 executes for 1 unit outside its critical section at time t_{15}, then locks local semaphore S_5 for 1 unit of time, and then executes for 1 unit of time before completing. The symbols in the table are as follows:

$C_{\text{non-cs}}$: Computation time of task outside all critical sections.

Parameters of Task Set of Example 3.4						
Task	Period	$C_{\text{non-cs}}$	C_{lcs}	C_{gcs}	C_{local}	U_{local}
τ_1	10	3	1	1	4	0.40
τ_3	20	4	1	1	5	0.25
τ_2	14	4	1	1	5	0.35
τ_4	27	3	3	1	6	0.22
τ_5	30	5	1	2	8	0.26
τ_6	40	3	1	2	6	0.15

Table 3-3: The Parameters of Task Set in Example 3.4

Worst-case Blocking Factors for Each Task					
Task	Factor 1	Factor 2	Factor 3	Factor 4	Total
τ_1	1	2	0	0	3
τ_3	0	2	4	0	6
τ_2	3	2	2	0	7
τ_4	0	2	7	0	9
τ_5	2	0	0	0	2
τ_6	0	0	0	0	0

Table 3-4: The Blocking Factors for Each Task
in Example 3.4

C_{lcs}: Computation time of task within critical sections guarded by local semaphores only.

C_{gcs}: Computation time of task within critical sections guarded by global semaphores only.

C_{local}: Computation time of task within its host processor excluding execution times on remote synchronization processors.

U_{local}: The utilization ratio given by $C_{\text{local}}/\text{Period}$.

The worst-case blocking duration of each task is the sum of 4 blocking factors given in Section 3.3.9. The following properties of the priority ceiling protocol are used to reduce the blocking factors. A job which suspends can be considered to be 2 jobs, only one of which is active at a time. The highest priority job in a processor will not be blocked by a local critical section if it does not access any semaphores. The lowest priority job on a processor encounters no local blocking either.

These blocking factors for each task are listed in Table 3-4. Blocking factor 1 is the upper bound on blocking from local lower priority critical sections and is determined as follows:

- Each instance of task τ_1 can be considered to be 2 jobs before and after its gcs execution. The first job encounters no local blocking, while the second job can encounter one blocking equal to τ_3's local critical section whose duration is 1.

- Instances of task τ_2 can also be considered to be two jobs. The second job can encounter one blocking equal to τ_4's lcs = 3.

- Tasks τ_3 and τ_4 encounter no local blocking.

- Tasks τ_5 and τ_6 always execute on processor $\wp_3$ and can therefore encounter only local blocking. By the priority ceiling protocol, τ_5 can encounter at most one blocking from $\tau_6 = max(2,1) = 2$. Task τ_6 encounters no blocking at all. Hence, the other blocking factors for τ_5 and τ_6 are all zero.

Blocking factor 2 is the upper bound on blocking from gcs's of lower priority tasks at remote processors. Since each global semaphore has its own priority ceiling and the priority ceiling protocol is used, a gcs z can block a job J_i' if the priority of J_i' is not greater than the priority ceiling of the global semaphore associated with z. This blocking factor is determined as follows.

- Task τ_1's gcs can be blocked by one of τ_2's gcs and τ_5's gcs. The maximum of these 2 critical sections has a duration of 2.

- Task τ_2's gcs can be blocked only by τ_5's gcs = 2.

- Task τ_3's gcs can be blocked by at most one gcs of the gcs's of τ_4, τ_5 and τ_6. The maximum blocking duration is therefore 2.

- Task τ_4's gcs can be blocked by at most one gcs of the gcs's of τ_5 and τ_6. The maximum blocking duration is therefore 2.

Schedulability Test Parameters					
Task	Period	C_{local}	U_{local}	B	C_{remote}
τ_1	10	4	0.40	3	1
τ_3	20	5	0.25	6	1
τ_2	14	5	0.35	7	1
τ_4	27	6	0.22	9	1
τ_5	30	8	0.26	2	0
τ_6	40	6	0.15	0	0
τ_1'	10	1	0.100	2	0
τ_2'	14	1	0.072	2	0
τ_3'	20	1	0.050	2	0
τ_4'	27	1	0.037	2	0

Table 3-5: The Schedulability Test Parameters for Each Processor of Example 3.4

Blocking factor 3 is the upper bound on remote blocking caused by the gcs's of higher priority tasks and is given by $CS_j * \lceil T_i/T_j \rceil$.

- Task τ_1 is the highest priority task and hence has no such blocking.

- Task τ_2 can be blocked by τ_1 and the blocking factor is given by $1 * \lceil 14/10 \rceil = 2$.

- Task τ_3 can be blocked by both τ_1 and τ_2, and the blocking factor $= 1 * \lceil 20/10 \rceil + 1 * \lceil 20/14 \rceil = 4$.

- Task τ_4 can be blocked by both τ_1, τ_2 and τ_3, and the blocking factor $= 1 * \lceil 27/10 \rceil + 1 * \lceil 27/14 \rceil 1 * \lceil 27/20 \rceil = 7$.

Blocking factor 4 is the upper bound on blocking caused by local execution of gcs's of lower priority tasks. Since there are no gcs's bound to $\wp_1$ and $\wp_2$, tasks τ_1 through τ_4 encounter no such blocking.

The total worst-case blocking for each task is given in the last column of Table 3-4. Now that the blocking factors have been determined, the next step is to determine whether each processor is schedulable. The scheduling parameters for these tests are listed in Table 3-5. The tests proceed as follows on processor 1.

- Task τ_1 executes locally for 4 units, remotely for 1 unit and has a blocking factor of 3 units. Hence, it will complete by 8 units and meet its deadline of 10.

- Task τ_3 executes locally for 5 units, remotely for 1 unit, and has a blocking factor of 6 units. It will also be preempted by the local execution of τ_1. Hence, we test whether

$$\frac{4}{10} + \frac{(5 + 1 + 6)}{20} \leq 1$$

and find that it is true. The utilization bound is 1 since the two tasks are harmonic. Hence τ_3 is schedulable.

The schedulability test on $\wp_2$ is as follows.

- Task τ_2 executes locally for 5 units, remotely for 1 unit, and has a blocking factor of 7 units. Hence, it will complete by 13 units and meet its deadline of 20.

- Task τ_4 executes locally for 6 units, remotely for 1 unit, and has a blocking factor of 9 units. It will also be preempted by the local execution of τ_2. Hence, we test whether

$$\frac{5}{14} + \frac{(6 + 1 + 9)}{27} \leq 2(2^{1/2} - 1)$$

and find that it is false. However, the exact characterization of Theorem 2-18 where one traces the critical zone shows that the task set is indeed schedulable:

$$(2 \times 5) + (6 + 1 + 9) = 26 \leq 27$$

The schedulability test on processor $\wp_3$ is slightly different and proceeds as follows.

- Since the execution requests for the gcs's of τ_1, τ_2, τ_3 and τ_4 would be regulated by the Period Enforcer, they would appear as periodic tasks of higher priority for tasks τ_5 and τ_6. The total utilization of these gcs's are given by $\frac{1}{10} + \frac{1}{14} + \frac{1}{20} + \frac{1}{27} = = 0.26$.

These gcs's have their own blocking factors as shown in Table 3-5, but since their utilization and blocking are low, it can easily be shown that they are schedulable.

- Task τ_5 executes for 8 units and has a blocking factor of 2 units. Hence, we test whether

$$0.26 + \frac{(8+2)}{30} \leq 5(2^{1/5}-1)$$

and find that it is true.

- Task τ_6 executes for 6 units and has no blocking factor. Therefore, we test whether

$$0.26 + \frac{8}{30} + \frac{6}{40} \leq 6(2^{1/6}-1)$$

and find that it is true.

We therefore conclude that the task set is schedulable with the 3 processors being utilized for 65%, 57% and 67% respectively. These utilizations may sound low, but $\wp_3$ is underutilized in this example. To improve utilization further, tasks with longer periods can be added to each processor, or global semaphore S_3 can be bound to a different processor. Also, one must note that such guaranteed timing behavior was not possible in previous protocols where there is no guarantee against unbounded blocking. Moreover, the timing constraints of our model are more stringent since a task must access a remote resource and perform computations all during the same period. Some loss of schedulability results from the fact that the task set assumes that the critical section durations are a very big fraction of the computational requirements of each task. Finally, the reason that the blocking factors are large is that blocking factor 3 is very pessimistic. However, it is possible to reduce this blocking factor by looking at the actual worst-case delay that will be encountered by a gcs request in terms of the critical zone at a synchronization processor.

3.4 TASK ALLOCATION

In this section, we illustrate a task allocation scheme to bind tasks to processors. The task allocation scheme is a complex optimization problem even for independent tasks [Dhall 78]. In reality, tasks do share data and

resources and the task allocation scheme must consider the blocking durations of each task to guarantee task deadlines. When the distributed
priority ceiling protocol is used, the blocking duration for each task is
bounded and should be considered by the task allocation scheme. Appropriate task binding goes a long way in minimizing remote blocking and
maximizing schedulability.

Traditional techniques for task allocation use graph-theoretic
methods [Shatz 87, Stone 77]. In this approach, the system is modeled as
a network in which tasks and processors are represented by nodes. Edges
between task nodes represent inter-processor communication costs while
edges between a task node and a processor node roughly represent the execution time. A graph-partitioning algorithm is then used to obtain a network cut with minimal weight. The complexity of this approach becomes
exponential when the system contains more than two processors. Such
graph partitioning algorithms cannot be used directly under our constraints. The methodology presented in [Stone 77], for instance, addresses
the assignment of tasks, all ready at the same time, to processors and
aims to minimize total execution times and communication times. In the
current scenario, where tasks are periodic, the task assignment problem is
not unlike a bin-packing problem [Coffman 83].

The objective of the task allocation would be to determine the smallest
number of processors which can schedule the tasks without missing deadlines. However, the determination of an optimal task allocation is beyond
the scope of this book and we shall just present an example of how the allocation could proceed:

Example 3.6: Let the set of tasks to be allocated be τ_1, τ_2, τ_3, τ_4,
and τ_5 arranged in descending order of their priorities as as-
signed by the rate-monotonic scheduling algorithm. Let the set
of semaphores in the system be S_1, S_2 and S_3. The tasks that
access these semaphores are pictorially represented in Figure
3-9(a), i.e. all the tasks access S_1, τ_3 and τ_4 access S_2, while τ_4
and τ_5 access S_3. However, τ_4's access of S_2 makes a nested access to S_3. Let us assume that at most two tasks can be
scheduled on a single processor. The blocking duration is minimum when tasks that access the same semaphore are allocated
to the same processor.

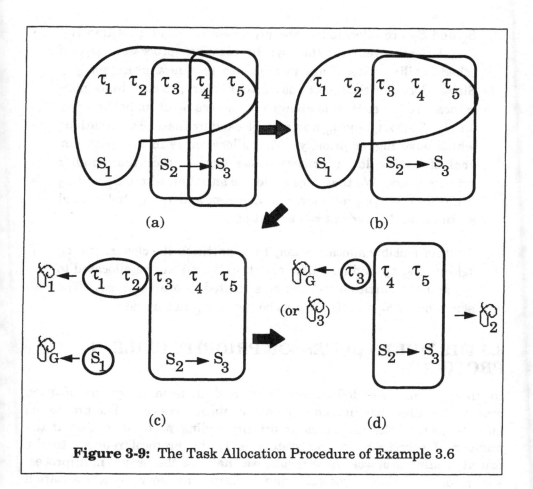

Figure 3-9: The Task Allocation Procedure of Example 3.6

Our objective is to separate these relationships to form "closures", tasks within which can then be allocated to the same processor. Since locks cannot be held across processors, the semaphores S_2 and S_3 have to be allocated to the same synchronization processor resulting in the representation of Figure 3-9(b). Since S_1 is accessed by all the tasks, S_1 can be allocated to a synchronization processor $\wp_G$. This leaves us with two closures comprising $\{\tau_1, \tau_2\}$ and $\{\tau_3, \tau_4, \tau_5\}$. We can now allocate τ_1 and τ_2 to the processor $\wp_1$, leaving a single closure. Since not all three tasks τ_3, τ_4 and τ_5 can be bound to the same processor, we need to partition the tasks. We partition them into $\{\tau_3\}$ and $\{\tau_4, \tau_5\}$. The latter partition along with the semaphores

S_2 and S_3 are allocated to the processor $\wp_2$. The partition $\{\tau_3\}$ can be allocated to the synchronization processor $\wp_G$ if schedulability criteria are met or else to a new processor $\wp_3$. Since global critical sections have higher priority than non-critical section code, this allows τ_3 to access S_2 at higher priority on $\wp_2$. Tasks τ_4 and τ_5 would be blocked by these gcs executions which have higher priority. This allocation is in line with our goal of having lower priority tasks block rather than higher priority tasks. We therefore avoid the situation where S_2 and S_3 are bound to τ_3's processor, and hence τ_4 and τ_5's global critical sections would preempt τ_3's execution.

Another feasible allocation may be to partition the closure $\{\tau_3, \tau_4, \tau_5\}$ into $\{\tau_3, \tau_4\}$ and $\{\tau_5\}$. The partition $\{\tau_3, \tau_4\}$ can be allocated to $\wp_2$ and the partition $\{\tau_5\}$ can be allocated to processor $\wp_G$. The semaphores S_2 and S_3 are also bound to $\wp_G$ in this case.

3.5 THE MULTIPROCESSOR PRIORITY CEILING PROTOCOL

In this section, we define, illustrate and analyze a synchronization protocol for direct use in shared memory multiprocessors. The protocol is an extension of the uniprocessor priority ceiling protocol in that if the number of processors in the system is 1, the protocol reduces to the priority ceiling protocol. As a result, we shall use the terms "multiprocessor priority ceiling protocol" and "shared memory synchronization protocol" interchangeably.

We assume that each processor in the system has its own local memory that holds all instructions and local data. Only global semaphores reside in shared memory and a cache if present is used only to minimize bus traffic during busy-waits to access global semaphore queues. The shared memory synchronization protocol to be outlined is used on each of the processors in the system. Recall that we assume that there are no nested or overlapping global critical sections. Under this protocol, resources guarded by local semaphores are accessed using the uniprocessor priority ceiling protocol locally on each processor, and globally shared resources are accessed using read-modify-write instructions such as test-and-set to obtain global semaphores.

3.5.1. Differences with the Distributed Protocol

The primary difference between the distributed and shared memory synchronization protocols is the processor where global critical sections are executed. In the distributed version, all global critical sections guarded by a semaphore are always executed on the same synchronization processor. In the shared memory protocol, a task's global critical sections are always executed on the host processor of the task. Hence, the gcs's corresponding to the same semaphore can be executed on different processors. The ability to lock global semaphores residing in shared memory makes this relatively very efficient in shared memory multiprocessors.

Another difference is the priorities at which gcs's need to execute under these two protocols. In the distributed priority ceiling protocol, a gcs guarded by a global semaphore S_G effectively executes at a priority equal to the global priority ceiling of S_G. In the multiprocessor priority ceiling protocol, not every gcs guarded by S_G needs to execute at the global priority ceiling of S_G. This is because of two reasons:

- A task's global critical sections now execute on its host processor.
- By Theorem 3-2, a gcs needs to execute at a higher priority than P_H only if it is blocking a task on a *remote* processor.

Consider a job J_i bound to $\wp$ which holds a lock on S_G. Let J' be the highest priority job on processors other than $\wp$ that can lock S_G. Then, using the same priority inheritance policy used in the distributed priority ceiling protocol, when J' blocks on S_G, J_i's gcs will execute at a maximum priority of $P_G + P'$. We refer to this priority as the *remote priority ceiling* of a gcs. If there exists a task τ on $\wp$ with higher priority than J' that can lock S_G, by Theorem 3-2, its gcs need not execute at a higher priority than this remote priority ceiling.

If a gcs guarded by S_G always executes at the priority level specified by its remote priority ceiling, its priority need not be changed dynamically since priority inheritance to the highest possible level occurs when the critical section is entered. Another important reason for this priority assignment is as follows. The worst-case blocking times obtained with the priority ceiling protocol where priority is inherited only after blocking occurs are identical to those obtained by *always* executing critical sections at the

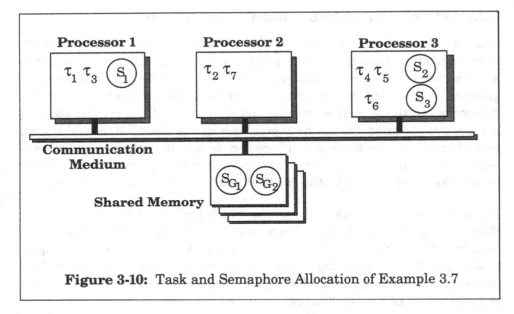

Figure 3-10: Task and Semaphore Allocation of Example 3.7

maximum possible priority value. Guaranteeing the deadlines of real-time tasks requires the worst-case conditions to be met. Hence this priority assignment scheme incurs no additional penalties, and a cheaper implementation becomes possible.

We illustrate this priority assignment scheme in the following example. The binding of tasks and semaphores to processors is illustrated in Figure 3-10.

Example 3.7: Consider the 3-processor configuration shown in Figure 3-10. Tasks τ_1 and τ_3 are bound to processor $\wp_1$, tasks τ_2 and τ_7 to processor $\wp_2$, and tasks τ_4, τ_5 and τ_6 to processor $\wp_3$. Jobs J_1 through J_7 execute the following sequence of steps:

$$J_1 = \{ \cdots, P(S_1), \cdots, V(S_1), \cdots, P(S_{G_1}), \cdots, V(S_{G_1}), \cdots \}$$
$$J_2 = \{ \cdots, P(S_{G_1}), \cdots, V(S_{G_1}), \cdots, P(S_{G_2}), \cdots, V(S_{G_2}), \cdots \}$$
$$J_3 = \{ \cdots, P(S_{G_1}), \cdots, V(S_{G_1}), \cdots, P(S_1), \cdots, V(S_1), \cdots \}$$
$$J_4 = \{ \cdots, P(S_2), \cdots, V(S_2), \cdots, P(S_{G_1}), \cdots, V(S_{G_1}), \cdots,$$
$$\quad P(S_2), \cdots, V(S_2), \cdots \}$$
$$J_5 = \{ \cdots, P(S_3), \cdots, V(S_3), \cdots, P(S_{G_2}), \cdots, V(S_{G_2}), \cdots \}$$
$$J_6 = \{ \cdots, P(S_2), \cdots, V(S_2), \cdots, P(S_3), \cdots, V(S_3), \cdots \}$$
$$J_7 = \{ \cdots, P(S_{G_2}), \cdots, V(S_{G_2}), \cdots \}$$

Semaphore	Priority Ceiling
S_1 (local)	$\mathsf{p}(J_1)$
S_2 (local)	$\mathsf{p}(J_4)$
S_3 (local)	$\mathsf{p}(J_5)$
S_{G_1} (global)	$P_G + \mathsf{p}(J_1)$
S_{G_2} (global)	$P_G + \mathsf{p}(J_2)$

Table 3-6: The Priority Ceilings of Semaphores in Example 3.7

Semaphores S_1 through S_3 can be held only by jobs bound to the same processor, and can therefore be bound to these processors as local semaphores. Thus, S_1 is a local semaphore on $\wp_1$, there are no local semaphores on $\wp_2$, and S_2 and S_3 are local semaphores on $\wp_3$. In addition, there are 2 global semaphores. Since the semaphores S_{G_1} and S_{G_2} can be held by jobs bound to different processors, these global semaphores must reside in shared memory.

Define the base priority ceiling P_G to be $\mathsf{p}(J_1) + 1$ as before. Recall that $\mathsf{p}(J_i) > \mathsf{p}(J_{i+1}).$ Then, the priority ceiling of each semaphore and the *normal* execution priority of each critical section are listed in Tables 3-6 and 3-7 respectively. Recall that a gcs always executes at the same priority (as specified by the remote priority ceiling of its semaphore), while an lcs may inherit the priority of a higher priority task.

3.5.2. The Definition of the Multiprocessor Priority Ceiling Protocol

The multiprocessor priority ceiling protocol is defined as follows.

1. A job uses its assigned priority unless it is within a critical section.

2. The uniprocessor priority ceiling protocol is used for all requests to local semaphores. This means the following:

   - When a job J requests the local semaphore S on processor $\wp$, let S^* be the semaphore with the highest

Job	Critical Section Guarded by	Normal Priority
J_1	S_1 S_{G_1}	$p(J_1)$ $P_G + p(J_2)$
J_2	S_{G_1} S_{G_2}	$P_G + p(J_1)$ $P_G + p(J_5)$
J_3	S_1 S_{G_1}	$p(J_3)$ $P_G + p(J_2)$
J_4	S_2 S_{G_1}	$p(J_4)$ $P_G + p(J_1)$
J_5	S_3 S_{G_2}	$p(J_5)$ $P_G + p(J_2)$
J_6	S_2 S_3	$p(J_6)$ $p(J_6)$
J_7	S_{G_2}	$P_G + p(J_5)$

Table 3-7: Normal Execution Priorities of Critical
Sections in Example 3.7

priority ceiling of all local semaphores locked by jobs
other than J on processor $\wp$.

- A job J on a processor $\wp$ can obtain the local
  semaphore S if its priority is higher than the priority
  ceiling of S^*. Else, J is said to be blocked by J^*. In this
  case, J^* inherits J's priority until it releases S^*.

- A job J can preempt another job J_L if its priority is
  higher than the priority, assigned or inherited, at
  which job J_L is executing.

3. A job J within a global critical section guarded by the global
   semaphore S_G has the priority assigned to its gcs.

4. A job J within a gcs can preempt another job J' within a gcs
   if the assigned priority of J's gcs is greater than that of J''s
   gcs.

5. When a job J requests a global semaphore S_G, S_G can be
   granted to J by means of an atomic transaction on shared
   memory, if S_G is not currently held by another job.

6. If a request for a global semaphore S_G cannot be granted, the job J is added to a prioritized queue on S_G without being preempted (i.e J holds the processor until it is inserted into the queue). The priority used as the key for queue insertion is the *normal* priority assigned to J.

7. When a job J attempts to release a global semaphore S_G, the highest priority job J_H waiting for S_G is signaled and becomes eligible for execution at J_H's host processor at its gcs priority. If there is no job suspended on S_G, the semaphore is released.

We illustrate the shared memory synchronization protocol using the task set presented in Example 3.7.

Example 3.8: The system configuration of the task set is shown in Figure 3-10. Consider the following sequence of events shown in Figure 3-11.

- At $t=0$, jobs J_3 and J_6 are the only jobs eligible for execution on processors $\wp_1$ and $\wp_3$ respectively, and begin execution. Processor $\wp_2$ remains idle.

- At $t=1$, J_3 locks global semaphore S_{G_1} on $\wp_1$ and begins execution at priority $= P_G+P_2$. Job J_2 begins execution on $\wp_2$. On $\wp_3$, J_6 locks local semaphore S_2 (since there are no other locked local semaphores).

- At $t=2$, J_1 arrives but is unable to preempt J_3 executing its gcs. Job J_2 continues execution on $\wp_2$ until $t=5$. Job J_4 arrives in $\wp_3$ and immediately preempts J_6 executing within its lcs.

- At $t=3$, J_3 releases the global semaphore S_{G_1} (since no other job is pending on the semaphore) and regains its original priority. As a result, J_1 preempts J_3 and begins execution on $\wp_1$. On $\wp_3$, J_4 attempts to lock the local semaphore S_2 but finds that its priority is not greater than the priority ceiling of the semaphore S_2 already locked by J_6. Hence, J_4 blocks, and J_6 resumes execution at the inherited priority of job J_4.

- At $t=4$, J_1 locks the global semaphore S_{G_1} on $\wp_1$. On $\wp_2$, J_7 arrives but is unable to preempt J_2 which continues execution. On $\wp_3$, J_6 releases S_2 and regains its low priority. Job J_4 preempts J_6 and is now able to lock S_2.

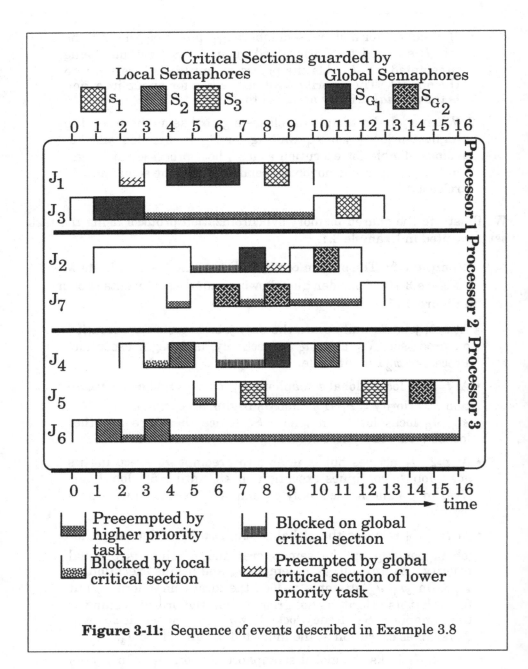

Figure 3-11: Sequence of events described in Example 3.8

- At $t=5$, J_1 continues execution of its gcs on $\wp_1$ until $t=7$. On $\wp_2$, J_2 attempts to lock S_{G_1} but is blocked since J_1 holds the semaphore. Hence, J_7 begins execution. On $\wp_3$, J_5 arrives but is unable to preempt J_4, which releases S_2 and continues execution.

- At $t=6$, J_2 is still blocked on $\wp_2$. Job J_7 locks the global semaphore S_{G_2} and begins execution of its gcs at priority $P_G + P_5$ (See Table 3-7). On $\wp_3$, J_4 attempts to lock S_{G_1} and is blocked. As a result, J_5 begins execution on $\wp_3$. Currently, J_2 and J_4 are both blocked on S_{G_1} and are queued in priority order on S_{G_1}.

- At $t=7$, J_1 performs a **V**() operation on S_{G_1}, and grants the semaphore to J_2, the highest priority job pending on it. Then, J_1 continues execution on $\wp_1$. On $\wp_2$, J_2 is eligible to execute its gcs with an execution priority of $P_G + P_1$ which is higher than J_7's gcs execution priority of $P_G + P_5$. Hence, J_2 preempts J_7 and begins execution of its gcs. On $\wp_3$, J_5 locks local semaphore S_3.

- At $t=8$, J_1 locks local semaphore S_1 on $\wp_1$. On $\wp_2$, J_2 needs to release S_{G_1} and grants the semaphore to J_4. Job J_2 also regains its normal priority and is preempted by the gcs of J_7. On $\wp_3$, J_4 enters its gcs at a high priority and preempts J_5.

- At $t=9$, J_1 releases S_1 and continues execution on $\wp_1$. On $\wp_2$, J_7 releases S_{G_2}, regains its lowest priority and is preempted by J_2. On $\wp_3$, J_4 releases S_{G_1}, regains its original priority and continues execution.

- At $t=10$, J_1 completes execution on $\wp_1$ and J_3 resumes execution. On $\wp_2$, J_2 locks global semaphore S_{G_2} and assumes its gcs priority. On $\wp_3$, J_4 attempts to lock S_2, and finds that its priority is higher than the priority ceiling of locked local semaphore S_3. Hence, J_4 is granted the semaphore and continues execution.

- At $t=11$, J_3 locks the local semaphore S_1, which it releases at $t=11$, and then completes at $t=12$ on $\wp_1$. On $\wp_2$, J_2 releases S_{G_2} and regains its original priority. On $\wp_3$, J_4 releases S_2 and continues execution.

- At $t=12$, J_2 and J_4 complete. Job J_7 resumes execution on $\wp_2$ while J_5 resumes execution of its lcs on $\wp_3$.

- Job J_5 releases S_3 at $t=13$, locks and releases global semaphore S_{G_2} at $t=14$ and $t=15$ respectively, and finally completes at $t=16$.

- Finally, J_6 can resume, lock and release S_3 and then complete on $\wp_3$.

Example 3.8 illustrates the following characteristics of the shared memory synchronization protocol. Jobs request and release local semaphores by using the uniprocessor priority ceiling protocol only on the local semaphores of each processor. Global semaphore requests do not follow any special protocol except that global critical sections execute at prespecified high priorities, and semaphore queues are priority-ordered. Any gcs executes at higher priority than all non-gcs code. Examples occur at $t=2$ on $\wp_1$ and $t=8$ on $\wp_2$. However, the gcs of one job can preempt the gcs of another if the execution priority of one gcs is higher than the execution priority of the other. An instance of this occurs at $t=7$ on $\wp_2$. Jobs suspended on a semaphore are signaled in priority order as at $t=7$. When a higher priority job suspends on a global semaphore, a lower priority job can execute on the processor as shown at $t=5$ on $\wp_2$.

The following blocking factors must be noted. While a job J on processor $\wp$ is blocked on a global semaphore, a lower priority job can lock a local semaphore on $\wp$. For example, J_5 locks S_3 on $\wp_3$ at $t=7$ after J_4 blocks on S_{G_1}. If this semaphore is later required or has a sufficiently high priority ceiling, J can be blocked by means of this semaphore later. Similarly, while J is blocked on a global semaphore, a lower priority job on $\wp$ can lock a global semaphore. For instance, J_7 locks S_{G_2} on $\wp_2$ at $t=6$ after J_2 blocks on S_{G_1}. Later, the global semaphore S_{G_2} is used by J_7 to preempt J_2 at $t=8$. This duration of preemption is additional waiting time imposed on J_2 due to high priority gcs execution of J_7. These two blocking factors can be avoided either by letting the processor idle when a job blocks on a global semaphore, or just by preventing any semaphore locks during this interval. However, both approaches can cause processor cycles to be lost which is generally unacceptable.

3.5.3. Determination of Task Blocking Times

In this section, we shall compute the worst-case waiting times that a job has to encounter before completion. The fundamental objective of the shared memory synchronization protocol is to obtain bounded waiting times for real-time tasks using shared memory primitives to access shared resources. The bounded waiting times in turn can be used to determine whether a set of real-time tasks running on a shared memory multiprocessor can meet their deadlines.

As in the case of the distributed priority ceiling protocol, the potential deferred execution of a task due to suspension on global semaphore accesses can cause a scheduling penalty. This scheduling penalty can result in a large factor that must be added to the worst-case blocking duration of a task. Again, the period enforcer technique [Rajkumar 91] must be used to eliminate this penalty. In this approach, the instants at which a task τ_i resumes execution must be separated by a minimum interval of T_i units of time. In addition, the instants at which requests for global semaphores are made must be separated by a minimum interval of T_i units of time. The illustration of the multiprocessor priority ceiling protocol in Example 3.8 does not use the period enforcement technique since only one instance of each task is used. However, we shall assume in the following that the period enforcer is used to avoid the stiff penalties of deferred execution.

It can be easily seen that the shared memory multiprocessor synchronization protocol prevents deadlocks. The uniprocessor priority ceiling protocol avoids deadlocks on local shared resources on each processor. In addition, by assumption, global critical sections do not nest other critical sections and vice-versa. The result follows.

<u>Remark</u>: If nested global critical sections are used, explicit partial ordering of global resources must be used to prevent deadlocks.

When a job J_i bound to a processor $\wp_j$ requests a global semaphore S_G, S_G can be held by a lower priority job J_k on a different processor $\wp_r$. However, the gcs of J_k can be preempted by a higher priority gcs on $\wp_r$. As a result, J_i can be blocked until this higher priority gcs completes on $\wp_r$ enabling J_k to resume and release S_G. Such a processor $\wp_r$ $(j \neq r)$ is called a *blocking processor* for J_i. In other words, a gcs on $\wp_r$ is assigned a higher priority than another gcs on $\wp_r$ guarded by S_G, and S_G will be requested by J_i on $\wp_j$.

In addition, we shall also use the following notation[19].

n_i^G: the Number of Global critical sections that a job J_i executes before its completion.

$NL_{i,j}$: The Number of jobs with Lower priority than J_i on processor $\wp_j$.

$\{J'_{i,r}\}$: The set of jobs on J_i's blocking processor $\wp_r$ with gcs's having higher priority than gcs's which can directly block J_i.

$NH_{i,r,k}$: The Number of gcs's of a job $J_k \in \{J'_{i,r}\}$ with Higher priority than a gcs on $\wp_r$ which can directly block J_i.

$\{GS_{i,k}\}$: The set of Global Semaphores each of which will be locked by both jobs J_i and J_k.

$NC_{i,k}$: The Number of global Critical sections entered by J_k and guarded by elements of $\{GS_{i,k}\}$.

The waiting time of a job J_i on processor $\wp_j$ (in addition to preemption by higher priority jobs on $\wp_j$) consists of several factors. We enumerate and bound each of these blocking factors below.

1. Each time J_i needs a global semaphore, it can potentially suspend, letting lower priority jobs execute on $\wp_j$. During this suspension, lower priority jobs can lock local semaphores. This locking can contribute to additional blocking to J_i when it resumes execution on $\wp_j$.

   At most n_i^G local critical sections of lower priority jobs can block a job J_i bound to a processor $\wp_j$. This follows from Corollary 2-13 and the fact that a job J_i can suspend itself when it attempts to enter a global critical section.

2. Each time J attempts to enter a gcs guarded by S_G, it can find that S_G is currently held by a lower priority job on a different processor.

   At most n_i^G global critical sections of lower priority jobs can block a job J_i bound to a processor $\wp$. This follows from the fact that semaphore queues are priority-ordered.

---

[19]Some predefined notation is repeated here for the sake of convenience.

3. Whenever J_i attempts to lock a global semaphore, it can always be preceded by higher priority jobs on other processors requesting the same semaphore. Global critical sections of higher priority jobs bound to $\wp_j$ itself can be considered to be normal preemption intervals for J_i.

At most $NC_{i,k} * \lceil T_i/T_k \rceil$ global critical sections of a higher priority job J_k bound to $\wp_r$ $(r \neq j)$ can block J_i on $\wp_j$. This follows directly from the fact that the number of instances of J_k within J_i's period is bounded by $\lceil T_i/T_k \rceil$, and each of J_k's $NC_{i,k}$ gcs executions can execute before J_i is granted a global semaphore. In a sense, this blocking factor can be considered to be the remote preemption penalty for a job. That is, higher priority jobs on remote processors which need the same resources can preempt J_i, and J_i needs to have sufficient slack to take these preemptions. The factor can be reduced by actually looking at the critical zone and computing the exact number of preemptions rather than the upper bound specified above.

4. Consider the set of blocking processors of J_i. Each of these processors contains higher priority gcs's which can preempt the gcs's of lower priority jobs directly blocking J_i.

For every $J_k \in \{J'_{i,r}\}$ on every blocking processor $\wp_r$, at most $NH_{i,r,k} * \lceil T_i/T_k \rceil$ gcs's can block J_i. This again follows from the argument that there can only be $\lceil T_i/T_k \rceil$ instances of J_k during one period of J_i. It is possible that $T_k > T_i$, i.e. a lower priority task's gcs has a higher priority than a gcs directly blocking τ_i's gcs. In this case, there can be 2 active instances of τ_k within τ_i's period. However, since the Period Enforcer technique is used, the gcs requests of τ_k will be separated by T_k units, and only 1 instance of τ_k can block τ_i. As a result, the ceiling of the ratio of the task periods yields the correct result.

5. Each time J_i needs a global semaphore, it can potentially suspend, letting lower priority jobs execute on $\wp$. During this suspension, lower priority jobs can lock or queue up on global semaphores. These global critical sections can execute at higher priority than P_H and can therefore preempt J_i when it executes non-gcs code.

At most $min(n_i^G+1, n_k^G)$ global critical sections of *every* job J_k with lower priority than J_i on processor $\wp_j$ can block J_i. This is due to the following. When J_i begins execution on $\wp_j$, a lower priority job J_k can have an outstanding request for a global semaphore. When this global semaphore is granted, J_k assumes higher priority than P_H within its gcs and can preempt J_i. This situation can repeat each time J_i suspends on a global semaphore. Hence, J_i can be blocked for at most $n_i^G + 1$ gcs's of J_k. In addition, since the period of a higher priority job J_i is shorter than the period of a lower priority job J_k ($i<k$) and the period enforcer is used, there can be at most one execution of J_k within J_i's period. As a result, J_k can enter at most n_k^G gcs's to block J_i within its period. The bound follows.

This blocking factor can be rather large but can be expected not to occur in practice. Each job needs to execute non-critical section code before entering new critical sections. As a result, not all critical sections of the lower priority jobs will be entered/requested during J_i's suspension(s). Thus, by considering actual time segments of execution of lower priority job, this blocking factor can be considerably reduced. In addition, there is some overlap between this blocking factor and the first two blocking factors above. For example, if a lower priority job is within an lcs, it cannot be within a gcs to block J_i. Also, the gcs's of lower priority jobs on J_i's host processor $\wp$ considered in this blocking factor need not be considered for inclusion in blocking factor 2.

Let B_i represent the worst-case waiting time that a job of a task τ_i can encounter. The term B_i for a task τ_i under the shared memory protocol is given by the sum of the above 5 blocking factors.

3.5.4. Schedulability Analysis

Once the worst-case waiting time of a job J_i has been determined, the schedulability analysis of the multiprocessor system can proceed on a processor-by-processor basis. On each processor, we now have a set of periodic tasks each of which can be preempted by higher priority tasks, and be blocked by the critical sections of lower priority tasks on the host processor and any task on other processors. This blocking factor was determined in the previous section. Again, Theorem 2-16 repeated as Theorem 3-7 can again be used to determine the schedulability of each processor. The set of inequalities in this theorem needs to be tested for each processor $\wp$ where n is the number of tasks bound to $\wp$, and C_k and T_k are the computation time and the period, respectively, of each task bound to $\wp$. The term B_i is the maximum duration that a job J bound to $\wp$ can be blocked from initiation to completion as discussed in the previous section.

3.5.5. A Schedulability Analysis Example

We illustrate the schedulability analysis of the multiprocessor priority ceiling protocol with the same task set that was used to illustrate the analysis of the distributed priority ceiling protocol in Section 3.3.10. The use of the same task set here serves to illustrate two points. First, it shows that it is possible to use either the multiprocessor or the distributed priority ceiling protocols on a given task set. Secondly, it shows how the total utilization is distributed across processors in these protocols. The example also illustrates how the blocking factors of Section 3.5.3 can be reduced with additional knowledge about the task set.

We assume that the binding of tasks to processors remains the same but since the protocol changes, gcs's are now executed on the host processors of tasks. Thus, the gcs's of tasks τ_1 and τ_3 execute on processor $\wp_1$, those of τ_2 and τ_4 execute on $\wp_2$, and those of τ_5 and τ_6 continue to execute on $\wp_3$.

The local and global priority ceilings of the semaphores are still given by Table 3-1. The next step is to assign the execution priorities to each of the global critical sections using their remote priority ceilings. These assignments are shown in Table 3-8. The periods and computation times within and outside critical sections for each task are the same as listed in Table 3-3.

The worst-case blocking duration of each task is the sum of 5 blocking factors given in Section 3.5.3. These blocking factors for each task are listed in Table 3-9. Blocking factor 1 is the upper bound on blocking from local lower priority critical sections and is identical to the distributed priority ceiling protocol except for τ_5.

- Each instance of task τ_1 can be considered to be 2 jobs before and after its gcs execution. The first job encounters no local blocking, while the second job can encounter one blocking equal to τ_3's local critical section whose duration is 1.

- Instances of task τ_2 can also be considered to be two jobs. The second job can encounter one blocking equal to τ_4's lcs = 3.

Normal Execution Priorities of Critical Sections		
Job	Critical Section Guarded by	Execution Priority
J_1	S_3	$P_G + \mathsf{p}(J_2)$
J_2	S_3	$P_G + \mathsf{p}(J_1)$
J_3	S_4	$P_G + \mathsf{p}(J_4)$
J_4	S_4	$P_G + \mathsf{p}(J_3)$
J_5	S_3	$P_G + \mathsf{p}(J_1)$
J_6	S_4	$P_G + \mathsf{p}(J_3)$

Table 3-8: The Execution Priorities of Global Critical Sections for Section 3.5.5

Worst-case Blocking Factors for Each Task						
Task	Factor 1	Factor 2	Factor 3	Factor 4	Factor 5	Total
τ_1	1	2	0	0	1	4
τ_3	0	2	0	4	0	6
τ_2	3	2	1	0	1	7
τ_4	0	2	1	5	0	8
τ_5	1	0	6	0	2	9
τ_6	0	0	4	7	0	11

Table 3-9: The Blocking Factors for Each Task in Section 3.5.5

- Tasks τ_3 and τ_4 encounter no local blocking.
- τ_5 can encounter one blocking from τ_6's lcs = 1.
- Task τ_6 encounters no local blocking.

Blocking factor 2 is the upper bound on *direct* blocking from gcs's of *lower* priority tasks from other processors and is determined as follows.

- Task τ_1 accesses S_3 only once but can be blocked by either τ_2 or τ_5 holding the semaphore from other processors. The maximum of these blocking durations is $max(1,2) = 2$.

- Task τ_3 accesses S_4 only once and can be blocked by either τ_4 or τ_6 holding the semaphore from other processors. The blocking factor is therefore $max(1,2) = 2$.

- Task τ_2's gcs can be blocked by either τ_1 or τ_5 holding the semaphore from other processors. However, τ_1 is a higher priority task. The blocking factor is therefore $= 2$.

- Task τ_4's gcs can be blocked by either τ_3 or τ_6, but τ_3 is a higher priority task. Hence, the blocking factor is $= 2$.

- Task τ_5's gcs is the lowest priority job accessing S_3, and hence this blocking factor is 0.

- Task τ_6's gcs is the lowest priority job accessing S_4, and has a blocking factor of 0.

Blocking factor 3 is the upper bound on *direct* remote blocking from gcs's of *higher* priority tasks from other processors and is determined as follows.

- Task τ_1 is the highest priority task accessing S_3 and hence this blocking factor is 0.

- Task τ_3 is the highest priority task accessing S_4 and hence this blocking factor is 0.

- Task τ_2 can be preceded by τ_1's gcs's and the upper bound to the blocking factor is given by $1 * \lceil 14/10 \rceil = 2$. However, we can use the critical zone argument here on the gcs's of τ_1 and τ_2 and find that τ_2's gcs will complete within 2 units, i.e. with a blocking (or remote preemption) of 1 unit from τ_1. Hence, this blocking factor is actually 1.

- Task τ_4 can be preceded by τ_3's gcs's and the blocking is given by $1 * \lceil 27/20 \rceil = 2$. In order to apply the critical zone argument, we must now consider the gcs's of τ_2, τ_3 and τ_4 since τ_4's gcs can be preempted by τ_2's gcs. It is easy to determine that τ_4's gcs will complete within 3 units and hence would have been preempted only once by τ_3's gcs. Hence, its blocking factor is actually 1.

- Task τ_5 can be preceded by the gcs's of both τ_1 and τ_2. Hence, the blocking is given by $1 * \lceil 30/10 \rceil + 1 * \lceil 30/14 \rceil = 6$.

- Task τ_6 can be preceded by the gcs's of both τ_3 and τ_4. Hence, the blocking is given by $1 * \lceil 40/20 \rceil + 1 * \lceil 40/27 \rceil = 4$.

Blocking factor 4 is the upper bound on the blocking introduced by higher priority gcs's from the blocking processors of a task. A blocking processor for a task τ_i contains higher priority gcs's which can preempt the gcs's of lower priority jobs directly blocking J_i. This blocking factor is computed as follows:

- Task τ_1 can be directly blocked by the gcs's of τ_2 and τ_5 on $\wp_2$ and $\wp_3$ respectively. However, both their gcs's have higher priority (P_G+P_1) than the other gcs's in their respective processors (which have priority P_G+P_3). Hence, τ_1 has no blocking processor and this blocking factor is 0.

- Similarly, it can be seen that tasks τ_2 and τ_5 have no blocking processors either. This is because both happen to access S_3 accessed by τ_1, the highest priority task in the system.

- Task τ_3's blocking processors are $\wp_2$ and $\wp_3$. This is because τ_3 can be blocked by the gcs's of τ_4 and τ_6 and they can be preempted by the gcs's of τ_2 and τ_5 respectively. Hence, this blocking factor is given by $1 * \lceil 20/14 \rceil + 2 * \lceil 20/30 \rceil = 4$.

- Task τ_4's blocking processors are $\wp_1$ and $\wp_3$. This is because τ_4 can be blocked by the gcs's of τ_3 and τ_6 and they can be preempted by the gcs's of τ_1 and τ_5 respectively. Hence, this blocking factor is given by $1 * \lceil 27/10 \rceil + 2 * \lceil 27/30 \rceil = 5$.

- Task τ_6's blocking processors are $\wp_1$ and $\wp_2$ because τ_6 can be blocked by the gcs's of τ_3 and τ_4 and they can be preempted by the gcs's of τ_1 and τ_2 respectively. Hence, this blocking factor is given by $1 * \lceil 40/10 \rceil + 1 * \lceil 40/14 \rceil = 7$.

Blocking factor 5 is the upper bound on blocking caused by local execution of gcs's of lower priority tasks. *Each* lower priority task can impose a blocking factor of at most $min(n_i^G+1, n_k^G)$ gcs's.

- Tasks τ_3, τ_4 and τ_6 are the lowest priority tasks on their respective processors, and hence they cannot encounter this blocking.

- Each of the other tasks τ_1, τ_2 and τ_5 can be blocked by at most 1 gcs of their lower priority tasks τ_3, τ_4 and τ_6 respectively. Their blocking factors are therefore $(1*1)=1$, $(1*1)=1$ and $(1*2)=2$ respectively.

Schedulability Test Parameters					
Task	Period	C_{local}	U_{local}	B	C_{remote}
τ_1	10	5	0.50	4	0
τ_3	20	6	0.30	6	0
τ_2	14	6	0.43	7	0
τ_4	27	7	0.26	8	0
τ_5	30	8	0.26	9	0
τ_6	40	6	0.15	11	0

Table 3-10: The Schedulability Test Parameters for Each Processor of Example 3.4

The total blocking factor for each task is the sum of the above 5 factors and is given in the last column of Table 3-9. Taking the sum is very pessimistic since mostly, if not always, the occurrence of one type of blocking means that another type of blocking cannot occur. However, the stochastic execution nature of tasks and the huge number of possible phasings is likely to render the procedure of determining any overlap very cumbersome.

Once the blocking factors have been determined, the schedulability of each processor can be tested with the parameters of Table 3-10. We immediately see that τ_1 on $\wp_1$ can complete 5 units of execution and 4 units of blocking within its period of 10, τ_2 on $\wp_2$ can complete 6 units of execution and 7 units of blocking within its period of 14, and τ_5 can complete 8 units of execution and 9 units of blocking within its period of 30.

Further analysis shows that τ_3 misses its deadline:

$5/10 + (6 + 6)/20 = 1.1 > 1.0$

The reason that τ_3 misses its deadline is because the total utilization of $\wp_1$ is 80%, a high load for a multiprocessor environment with global resource-sharing requirements. In order to make τ_3 schedulable, τ_3's execution time can be reduced to 4, or its period needs to be extended to 27. Then, the total utilization of $\wp_1$ will be 70% in the former case and 72% in the latter instead of the current 80%.

On $\wp_2$, τ_4 meets its deadlines because in its critical zone, two instances of τ_2 occur and we have

$\quad$ $(2\times6) + 7 + 8 = 27 \leq 27$

The total utilization of the processor is 69%.

On $\wp_3$, τ_6 also meets its deadline because two instances of τ_5 occur in its critical zone and we have,

$\quad$ $(2\times8) + 6 + 11 = 33 < 40$

As can be seen, there is more slack that can be utilized on this processor and the total utilization of the processor is just 41%.

The schedulability analysis shows that τ_3 does not meet its deadlines on $\wp_1$ since the distribution of the system utilization is very non-uniform with 80% on $\wp_1$, 69% on $\wp_2$ and 41% on $\wp_3$. Hence, this example demonstrates that the multiprocessor priority ceiling protocol is not the right protocol for this particular task allocation, and a different task allocation with more uniform distribution of system utilization is necessary.

3.5.6. Comparison of Multiple Processor Synchronization Protocols

Under the distributed synchronization protocol described in Section 3.3, all global critical sections guarded by a global semaphore S_G must be executed on the same synchronization processor. The first 2 blocking factors of the multiprocessor priority ceiling protocol have their virtually identical counterparts under the distributed synchronization protocol as well. Its third and fourth blocking factors tend to be distributed between the third and fourth blocking factors of the distributed protocol. The fourth blocking factor can be reduced in the distributed priority ceiling protocol by adding more synchronization processors, but the shared memory protocol can use these extra processors as additional processing resources.

The principal advantage of the distributed protocol is that it allows gcs's to be nested as long as locks do not cross processor boundaries. This becomes possible because all gcs's guarded by the same semaphore are bound to the same processor. Under the shared memory protocol, the blocking factors rise rapidly when global critical sections are nested. Also, as can be seen by the analyses in Section 3.3.10 and 3.5.5, the worst-case blocking duration of a task tends to be higher for the multiprocessor protocol than in the distributed protocol. These disadvantages of the shared memory protocol have to be weighed against its higher implementation efficiency in tightly coupled multiprocessors. In contrast, there is a relatively large overhead inherent in the distributed protocol where every gcs of a job is generally executed in a remote processor and communication delays must be added to the task blocking factors.

3.5.7. Implementation Considerations

The local priority ceiling protocol can be implemented as discussed in Section 2.4.3. The principal additional requirements of the shared memory synchronization protocol lie at the entry and exit points to global critical sections. Associated with each global semaphore is also a data structure in shared memory which represents a priority-ordered queue of tasks that suspend on the semaphore. This queue becomes part of the globally shared data structure which can be guarded by a user-transparent semaphore S_u. Any operations to this semaphore queue must be atomic as well. This is enforced as follows. Before a task enters a global critical section, it must first obtain the global semaphore S_G associated with the gcs.

When a task needs to lock S_G, it first busy-waits, locks S_u using a read-modify-write operation in the shared memory space and then accesses S_G. If the P() operation is successful, it releases S_u. Else, if S_G is currently held by another task, the task queues itself on the semaphore queue and releases S_u. To avoid the generation of excessive traffic on the backplane during any busy-wait, the task spin-reads its own cache entry until S_U is released [Dubois 88]. A task releasing a global semaphore first obtains the semaphore S_U (with a busy-wait if necessary), picks the highest priority task off the queue (if any), awakens the task and transfers to it the lock on S_G. If there are no tasks pending, it releases S_G. Finally, it releases S_U. Also, a task is non-preemptable while it performs a busy-wait on the semaphore S_u. This is such that task awakening and queueing are not unnecessarily postponed. The duration of busy-wait should be relatively short since it represents only the duration of adding an entry to (or deleting an entry from) a linked list and testing S_G.

As can be seen, the cache and the cache-coherence scheme specified in the system configuration are used only for avoiding the generation of unnecessary bus traffic while performing a busy-wait on locks to semaphore queues. Another configuration is possible if an interprocessor interrupt mechanism is available. Then, the cache, the cache coherence requirement and the busy-wait situation can be replaced as follows. When a job needs to busy-wait, it does not relinquish the processor but records its status in a field within the lock and disables all interrupts except interprocessor interrupts. The job and the processor suspend until an interprocessor interrupt arrives [Dubois 88].

3.5.8. Variations in the Multiprocessor Priority Ceiling Protocol

Variations in the multiprocessor priority ceiling protocol protocol defined in Section 3.5.2 are possible. An important variation of the shared memory prioritized synchronization protocol attempts to reduce the considerable blocking factor 5, where every lower priority job can lock or queue up on a global semaphore when a higher priority job is suspended on a global semaphore.

One approach is as follows: while a higher priority job J_i on a processor $\wp$ is suspended on a global semaphore, a lower priority job J_j is not allowed to block on any global semaphore. However, J_j is allowed to lock S_G' if it is unlocked at the moment of request. If the request for S_G cannot be satisfied immediately, J_j does not block on the semaphore queue. Instead, J_j suspends itself on $\wp$ and will retry the operation later. If the processor becomes idle during this process, jobs which have suspended themselves can retry their operations in priority order. If job J_j obtains the lock S_G, its gcs will execute at a priority higher than P_H and cannot be preempted by other tasks with lower priority than J_i. As a result, when J_i resumes, it can find at most one lower priority job within a gcs after J_i's resumption. Thus, J_i can be blocked for at most one gcs of a lower priority task whenever it suspends. This scheme reduces the blocking time of J_i dramatically. However, it adds a relatively large blocking factor for J_j, which is given by the maximum time that J_i would take to begin its gcs. Hence, this variation can be used selectively on some tasks to reduce their blocking factors in order to enable them to meet their deadlines.

The shared memory protocol does not change when global critical sections are nested inside one another. However, deadlocks need to be explicitly avoided, say, by imposing a partial ordering of resources. The blocking durations with nested critical sections can then become a major schedulability bottleneck. Also, the blocking factors for the protocol listed above are true only for non-nested global critical sections. This is because each nested global critical section not only increments n_i^G but can also rapidly increase the number of blocking processors via a transitive relationship. For instance, a job J holding a global semaphore on one processor can block on a nested semaphore held on a second processor by another job, which in turn is blocked on another nested semaphore and so on. As a result, the list of blocking processors for the first job can include the list for the second job etc. In general, blocking factors 2, 3 and 4 scale up with nested critical sections. Another possible approach to analyze nested gcs's is to collapse nested critical sections into non-nested gcs's. This can be done by introducing semaphores which subsume the nested semaphores. For instance, a database transaction requiring two distinct objects may obtain two locks. Instead, a lock which provides access to both objects can be introduced. This is analogous to locking a larger section of the database for each transaction.

3.6 SUMMARY

Multiple processor systems have become popular due to the expected saturation of uniprocessor speeds and the potential speedup possible from the use of several processors. Unfortunately for real-time systems, the unbounded priority inversion problem in the uniprocessor domain becomes much more severe when multiple processors run tasks which share logical and physical resources among them. Hence, the problem of unbounded waiting time for access to global resources on multiple processor systems must be addressed. The priority ceiling protocol is an efficient synchronization protocol for uniprocessors that not only prevents deadlocks but also limits the blocking duration of a task to at most the duration of one critical section of a lower priority task. The distributed priority ceiling protocol is an extension of the priority ceiling protocol that can be applied to tasks executing in parallel on multiple processor systems. This protocol prevents deadlocks and bounds the duration that a task has to wait for access to global data and/or resources. A task allocation scheme is to be used to bind tasks to processors. Since the task allocation is determined off-line, the complexity of the allocation algorithm need not be a dominating factor in order to achieve a schedulable configuration with a small number of processors.

The distributed priority ceiling protocol uses a remote procedure call model and can be easily implemented since each processor in the system merely implements the uniprocessor priority ceiling protocol locally on its processor. The only difference is that some execution threads are assigned higher priorities. This allows the protocol to be supported well, for example, under the semantics of Ada in a system with multiple processors.

The shared memory multiprocessor synchronization protocol is designed for use in tightly-coupled multiprocessors where shared memory transactions can be implemented very efficiently. The properties of this protocol allow us to derive a set of sufficient conditions to determine whether real-time tasks using this protocol can meet their timing constraints. Finally, we have compared its merits and demerits with respect to the distributed priority ceiling protocol. The properties of these protocols allow the derivation of sufficient conditions to test whether the deadlines of a given task set can be met. In addition, the shared memory and distributed protocols can be mixed to reduce critical blocking factors and/or support nested critical sections.

Chapter Four

Distributed Real-Time Databases

4.1 INTRODUCTION

4.1.1. Motivation

Real-time databases are used in a wide range of applications such as aircraft tracking and the monitoring and control of modern manufacturing facilities. In a real-time database context, concurrency control protocols must not only maintain the consistency constraints of the database but also satisfy the timing requirements of the transactions accessing the database. In standard database applications, such as banking, one can lock data objects and prevent other transactions from accessing them in order to maintain consistency. In a real-time application such as tracking, the consistency is still important, but it is also critical that the values of the data objects are timely. If an object being tracked is moving fast, very stringent timing requirements will be placed on transactions that update the object location. Failure to meet these timing requirements will render the tracking exercise a failure, because the data will be out of date.

To satisfy both the consistency and real-time constraints, we need to integrate concurrency control protocol with real-time scheduling protocols. In this chapter, we focus on the integration of a locking concurrency protocol with a static priority real-time scheduling protocol, since both these two types of protocols are widely used in practice. A major source of problems in integrating the two protocols is the lack of coordination in the development of concurrency control protocols and of real-time scheduling protocols. Owing to the effect of blocking due to concurrency control, a direct application of a real-time scheduling algorithm to tasks (transactions) may result in unbounded priority inversion, described in Chapter 2, where a higher priority task is blocked by lower priority tasks for an indefinite period of time. Consequently, the management of task priorities during task synchronization is a major issue in our investigation. On the other hand, in the design of concurrency control protocols, it is often assumed that the more concurrency offered by the protocol, the better is the performance. For example, the two-phase locking protocol [Eswaran 76]with read and write semantics is considered to be superior than two phase lock protocol using exclusive locks. However, as we will see in Section 4.2.2, a direct application of the read and write semantics can actually lead to poorer schedulability[20]. The sharing of a read-lock can improve real-time performance only if certain conditions regarding the priorities of readers and writers are satisfied. In this chapter, we will address these issues arising from the integration of a concurrency control protocol with a real-time scheduling protocol. However, before we address the integration issues, we give a brief review of the concurrency control protocol and the real-time scheduling protocol that we aim to integrate.

4.1.2. Related Work

Concurrency control [Attar 84, Beeri 83, Bernstein 79, Garcia-Molina 83, Lynch 83, Mohan 86, Papadimitriou 86, Schwarz 84, Weihl 83]   is an active area of research as is real-time scheduling theory. It is beyond the scope of this book to examine the possible combinations of concurrency control and real-time scheduling protocols. Rather, we limit ourselves to the integration of two particular protocols: the rate monotonic scheduling algorithm [Liu 73] and the modular concurrency control protocol [Sha 88].

The modular concurrency control protocol [Sha 88] offers reduced blocking time through the decomposition of the database and the transactions. This decomposition approach has two aspects. First, data objects in the database are decomposed into disjoint sets called *atomic data sets*(ADS). The consistency of each atomic data set can be maintained independent of the other atomic data sets. The union of atomic data sets is still an atomic data set, and the conjunction of the consistency constraints of all the atomic data sets is assumed to be equivalent to the consistency constraints of the database. Secondly, each transaction is decomposed into a partially ordered set of *elementary transactions* and *tasks*. The entire transaction is called a *compound transaction*. The model of a compound transaction in this theory allows us to address the real-time scheduling of a mixture of

---

[20]Schedulability is the level of processor utilization at or below which the deadlines of a set of periodic tasks can always be met.

non-database operations, *elementary tasks*, and database-accessing activities, *elementary transactions*, in a single task.[21] Each of the elementary transactions in a compound transaction maintains the consistency of the accessed atomic data set when executing alone on the set. In addition, the post-condition of the compound transaction is assumed to be equivalent to the conjunction of the post-conditions of the elementary tasks and transactions of a compound transaction in any execution path. Since compound transaction is a model of our tasks, we will use the terms "tasks" and "compound transactions" interchangeably in the following discussions. Having decomposed the database and the transactions, we use the setwise two phase lock protocol[22] to make sure that elementary transactions are run serializably with respect to each of the atomic data sets. It was shown in [Sha 88] that the resulting schedules form a superset of sets of serializable schedules. In addition, these schedules possess the properties of consistency, correctness and modularity. Compound transactions and atomic data sets provide us with a useful model for real-time database applications such as tracking, and we illustrate their application in the following example.

Suppose that an airplane is being tracked by two radar stations, and the collection of data objects, O_1 and O_2, represent the local views of these two stations. These data objects might include the current location, velocity, and identification of the airplane as seen by the particular station. Each of these two data objects forms an atomic data set. This is because the consistency constraints associated with each track can be checked and validated locally. Each new scan creates a new version of the data object,

---

[21]Although the original theory [Sha 88] did not address non-database operations, non-database operations such as data-processing tasks can be viewed as a special elementary transaction which locks some dummy data object that no other transaction will either read or write. Hence, no special treatment is needed from a concurrency control point of view. However, from a real-time scheduling point of view, it is important to distinguish the data processing and the database operations, because an elementary task will always be preempted by the execution of higher priority tasks, but an elementary transaction can block the execution of higher priority ones. The blocking of high priority tasks, as we will see, has important implications to the schedulability of a real-time system.

[22]Under this protocol, a transaction cannot release any lock on any atomic data set until it has obtained all the locks on that atomic data set. Once it has released a lock on any atomic data set, it cannot obtain a new lock on that atomic data set. The transaction can, however, obtain new locks on other atomic data sets.

and in the course of time, the values of O_1 and O_2 form two correlated multivariate time series. The correlation can be used to create a new atomic data set consisting of the global track, represented by data object O_3. The global ADS, i.e., the union $G = \{O_1, O_2, O_3\}$, represents the global and local views of the airplane being tracked.

The notion of atomic data sets is especially useful for tracking multiple targets. Before the formation of the global atomic data sets, we need to correlate all the local tracks near each other to find out which tracks are associated with which targets. Once a global ADS associated with a particular target is formed, the information from the global track can be referenced as a global context to aid the local operations. In addition, the knowledge of a set of local tracks belonging to the same global ADS helps to reduce the number of correlation operations. When data from new scans are used to update the local tracks of a global ADS, we will correlate them first. If the correlation is successful, then the hypothesis that all the ADS's in G are tracking the same target is considered to be valid and there is no need to further correlate the data with the tracks from other ADS's. This may substantially reduce the computation time required in tracking.[23] Conceptually, the birth (the creation of a global track), growth (adding/deleting local ADS's in G) and death (the global track is invalidated by new discoveries) of global ADS's model the dynamics of a tracking database.

In real-time tracking applications, an instance of a periodic task consists of both non-database operations and database operations. In fact, the non-database operations such as signal processing is often more time-consuming than reading and writing the tracks in the database. The structure of a compound transaction provides a useful model for such tasks. To illustrate the syntax of a compound transaction, consider a simple distributed tracking database consisting of a global database GD and a set of local databases LD_1, ..., LD_n. Each local database is as-

---

[23]It is important to emphasize that while the ADS's in G are linked by correlation, the degree of correlation is not a consistency constraint. Consistency constraints are relationships between data objects that must be maintained by all the transactions. On the other hand, transactions do not have any responsibility to maintain the correlation between the ADS's in G. In fact, if the initial correlation is due to some signal processing error, then the global ADS will become invalid and must be eliminated, the sooner the better.

sociated with a particular sensor, and the data from the sensor is
processed to create local tracks. Compound transaction Global_View
reads the local tracks of a global ADS, correlates them and then updates
the global track if the correlation is successful. The pseudo-code of the
transaction *Global_View* is given in Figure 4-1.

```
Compound_Transaction Global_View;
AtomicVariable obj_new_vector: Track_Vector;
BeginSerial
    BeginParallel
        Elementary_Transaction Read_Local_ADS_1
        BeginSerial
            Lock Lock_Track_1;
            obj_new_vector := Local_Track_1;
            Commit and Unlock Local_Track_1
        EndSerial;

            ...

        Elementary_Transaction Read_Local_ADS_n
        BeginSerial

            ...

        EndSerial

    EndParallel;

    Elementary_Task
    BeginSerial
      Correlate data in obj_new_vector;
    EndSerial;

    If correlation_successful Then
    Begin
        Elementary_Transaction Global_View
        BeginSerial
            Lock  Global_Track;
            Update Global_Track;
            Commit and Unlock Global_Track;
        EndSerial;
    End;
    Else Begin
        Correlate the data with nearby
                    tracks from other ADS's
    End;
EndSerial;
```

Figure 4-1: The Pseudo-Code For a Tracking Transaction *Global_View*.

This example illustrates the following characteristics of our approach. The database is decomposed, and the compound transaction models a generalized task which has both database and non-database operations. In addition, elementary transactions are executed serializably with respect to the atomic data sets.[24]

The rest of the chapter is organized as follows. In Section 4.2.1, we examine the priority inversion problem that must be solved in the development of a real-time concurrency control protocol. In Section 4.2.2, we develop the *read-write (rw) priority ceiling* protocol for real-time concurrency control in the context of a centralized database. In Section 4.3, we address the real-time concurrency control problem in a distributed environment. Finally, Section 4.4 summarizes our results.

4.2 REAL-TIME CONCURRENCY CONTROL ISSUES

4.2.1. The Priority Inversion Problem

The major bottleneck in integrating a locking protocol with a priority driven scheduling protocol is again the problem of priority inversion, which is inevitable in transaction systems. However, to achieve a high degree of schedulability in real-time applications, we must overcome the problem of uncontrolled priority inversion, where the priority inversion occurs over an indefinite period of time. This is illustrated by the following example, which is identical to Example 2.1 but is recast in database terminology:

> **Example 4.1:** Suppose τ_1, τ_2 and τ_3 are three tasks arranged in descending order of priority with τ_1 having the highest priority. Assume that elementary transactions T_1 of task τ_1 and T_3 of τ_3 access the same data object O. Suppose that at time t_1 transaction T_3 obtains a write-lock on O. During the execution of T_3, the high priority task τ_1 arrives, preempts T_3 and later attempts to execute T_1 to access the object O. Task τ_1 will be blocked, since O is already locked. We would expect that τ_1, being the

---

[24]The atomic variables are global variables of a compound transaction and are shared by the elementary transactions and tasks.

highest priority task, will be blocked no longer than the time for transaction T_3 to complete and unlock O. However, the duration of blocking may, in fact, be unpredictable. This is because transaction T_3 can be preempted by the intermediate priority task τ_2 that does not need to access O. The blocking of T_3, and hence that of τ_1, will continue until τ_2 and any other pending intermediate priority level tasks are completed. This blocking duration can be arbitrarily long.

Our objective is to design an appropriate priority management protocol for a given concurrency control protocol so that deadlocks can be avoided and the duration of blocking is tightly bounded. Again, the use of priority inheritance is one approach to bound the arbitrary delays caused by a locking protocol. As discussed in Chapter 2, the basic idea of priority inheritance is that when a task τ's transaction T blocks higher priority tasks, it executes its elementary transaction at the highest priority of all the transactions blocked by T.

We develop below the *rw_priority ceiling protocol*, which not only minimizes the blocking time of a task τ to the duration of at most one elementary transaction but also prevents the formation of deadlocks. Similar to the priority ceiling protocol, the underlying idea of this protocol is to ensure that when a transaction T preempts another transaction, the priority at which this new transaction will execute must be guaranteed to be strictly higher than the priorities of all the preempted transactions, taking the priority inheritance protocol into consideration. If this condition cannot be satisfied, transaction T is suspended, and the transaction that blocks T inherits T's priority. Example 4.2 illustrates this idea and the deadlock avoidance property of this protocol.

We define the *write priority ceiling* of a data object as the priority of the highest priority transaction that may write-lock this object. We also define the *absolute priority ceiling* of a data object as the priority of the highest priority object that can either read-lock or write-lock this object. The *rw_priority ceiling* of an object O represents the highest priority task that a transaction that has locked only O can inherit. When a transaction T write-locks the object, T can block all transactions requiring access to O, and hence the rw_priority ceiling of the object is considered to be its absolute priority ceiling. Conversely, when a transaction T read-locks the object, T can block all write transactions and the rw_priority ceiling of O becomes its write priority ceiling. A transaction will be granted a lock on a semaphore only if its priority is strictly higher than the current rw_priority ceilings of all objects locked by other transactions.

Example 4.2: Suppose that we have three tasks τ_0, τ_1 and τ_2 arranged in descending order of priority. In addition, there are two data objects O_1 and O_2 belonging to the same ADS A.

Suppose the sequences of processing steps for the transactions embedded in the three tasks are as follows:

$$\tau_0 = \{ \cdots, \ \textit{Write-Lock}(O_0), \ \cdots, \ \textit{Unlock}(O_0), \ \cdots \}$$

$$\tau_1 = \{ \cdots, \ \textit{Read-Lock}(O_1), \ \cdots, \ \textit{Write-Lock}(O_2), \ \cdots, \\ \textit{Unlock}(O_2), \ \cdots, \ \textit{Unlock}(O_1), \ \cdots \}$$

$$\tau_2 = \{ \cdots, \ \textit{Read-Lock}(O_2), \ \cdots, \ \textit{Write-Lock}(O_1), \ \cdots, \\ \textit{Unlock}(O_1), \ \cdots, \ \textit{Unlock}(O_2), \ \cdots \}$$

The sequence of events described below is depicted in Figure 4-2.

First, we establish the priority ceiling of each of the data objects. The write_priority ceiling and absolute priority ceiling for data object O_1 are the priorities of tasks τ_2 and τ_1, P_2 and P_1, respectively. For data object O_2, both the write and absolute priority ceilings are equal to P_1. For data object O_0, both ceilings are equal to P_0.

Suppose that at time t_0, task τ_2 starts its execution. At time t_1, τ_2 has executed Read-Lock(O_2) and the rw_priority ceiling of O_2 is set at the write_priority ceiling of O_2, i.e., P_1. Having locked O_2, task τ_2 starts executing its embedded transaction T_2. At time t_2, task τ_1 is initiated and preempts transaction T_2. However, when task τ_1 tries to execute its embedded transaction at time t_3 by making an indivisible system call to execute Read-Lock(O_1), the scheduler will find that task τ_1's priority P_1 is *not* higher than the rw_priority ceiling of *locked* data object O_2, which was set at P_1. Hence, the scheduler suspends transaction τ_1 without letting it read-lock O_1. Note that τ_1 is blocked

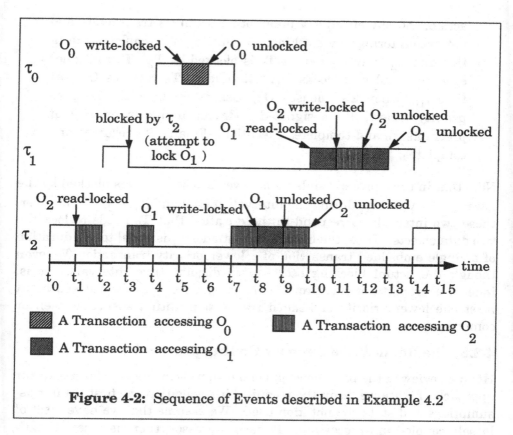

Figure 4-2: Sequence of Events described in Example 4.2

outside its embedded transaction. Transaction T_2 now *inherits* the priority of task τ_1 and resumes execution. Since τ_1 is denied the read-lock on O_1 and suspended instead, a potential deadlock between T_1 and T_2 is prevented. If τ_1 were granted the read-lock on O_1, then τ_1 would later wait for τ_2 to release the read-lock on O_2, while τ_2 would wait for τ_1 to release the read-lock on O_1.

On the other hand, suppose that at time t_4, while T_2 is still in its transaction, the highest priority task τ_0 arrives and attempts to write-lock data object O_0 at time t_5. Since the priority of τ_0 is higher than the rw_priority ceiling of locked data object O_2, task τ_0's transaction T_0 will be granted the write-lock on the data object O_0. Task τ_0 will therefore continue and execute its transaction, thereby effectively preempting T_2 in its transaction and not encountering any blocking. At time t_7, T_0 completes execution and T_2 is awakened for T_1 is blocked by T_2. T_2 continues execution and write-locks O_1. At time t_9, T_2 releases O_1. At time t_{10}, when T_2 releases O_2, task τ_2 resumes its assigned priority. Now, T_1 is signaled. Having a higher priority, it preempts T_2 and completes execution. Finally, T_2 resumes and completes.

Note that in the above example, τ_0 is never blocked. τ_1 was blocked by the lower priority task τ_2 during the intervals $[t_3, t_4]$ and $[t_7, t_{10}]$[25]. However, these two intervals correspond to the duration that T_2 needs to lock the two data objects. Thus, the blocking duration of τ_1 is equal to the duration of a single embedded transaction of a lower priority transaction T_2, even though the actual blocking occurs over disjoint time intervals. It is, indeed, a property of this protocol that any task τ can be blocked by at most one lower priority embedded transaction until τ suspends itself or completes.

4.2.2. The Read-Write Priority Ceiling protocol

Having reviewed the basic concepts of our approach, we now formalize our approach. Before we begin the technical investigation, we first list our assumptions and state the notation used. We assume that we have a set of loosely coupled uni-processors. In each processor, there is a set of statically allocated periodic tasks. A task can execute in parallel on more than one processor. For example, task τ can update an ADS and its replication on processors X and Y in parallel. We assume that each stream of aperiodic tasks, if any, will be converted to periodic activities via a periodic server task. For example, to handle random requests from an operator, we can buffer his input and use a periodic server task to respond to his requests periodically[26]. Since tracking operations consist of both signal processing and database accessing, we assume that each instance of a

---

[25]The interval $[t_3, t_4]$ is not considered blocking for τ_1 since it was only preempted by the higher priority task τ_0.

[26]For an advanced treatment of aperiodic tasks, readers are referred to [Lehoczky 87b].

periodic task is an interleaving of data-processing code and database operations modeled as elementary tasks and elementary transactions of a compound transaction respectively. We shall assume that the database is decomposed into atomic data sets, and the setwise two-phase lock protocol is used by elementary transactions for concurrency control. We assume that the rate-monotonic algorithm is used to assign a priority to each task. If two tasks are ready to run on a processor, the higher priority task will run. Equal priority tasks are run in a FCFS order. We also assume that a transaction does not attempt to lock an object that it has already locked and thus deadlock with itself. In addition, we assume that in each processor the runtime system will serialize the execution of syntactically parallel elementary tasks and transactions. For example, in a uni-processor if a compound transaction has the construction

```
  . . .
BeginParallel
        Elementary_Transaction_1;
        Elementary_Transaction_2;
EndParallel
  . . .
```

then either Elementary_Transaction_1 completes before the start of Elementary_transaction_2, or vice versa. These two elementary transactions will, of course, execute in parallel, should they execute on different processors. A task can suspend itself during its execution of non-database operations, e.g. waiting for I/O. However, self suspension is not permitted when it holds locks on database objects. This also implies that we do not permit a transaction to lock across the network. We also assume that either multiple "read" locks or a single "write" lock can be held on a data object.

Notation: We use the notation $\{A_1, \cdots, A_k\}$ to denote the atomic data sets of database D.

Notation: We denote the given tasks as an ordered set $\{\tau_1, \cdots, \tau_n\}$ where the tasks are listed in descending order of priority, with τ_1 having the highest priority.

Notation: We use $T_{i,j}$ to denote an elementary transaction of task τ_i that accesses ADS A_j. We will also use the simplified notation T_i when the identity of the ADS is not important.

Notation: We use the notation P_i to denote the priority of task τ_i.

Definition: The lock on a data object can either be a read-lock or a write-lock. A task τ that holds a read-lock (write-lock) on a data object O is said to have read-locked (write-locked) object O. The *write priority ceiling* of a data object is defined as the highest priority task that may write this object. The *absolute priority ceiling* of a data object is defined as the highest priority task that may read or write this object. When a data object O is write-locked, the *rw_priority ceiling* of O is defined to be equal to the absolute priority ceiling of O. When a data object O is read-locked, the rw_priority ceiling of O is defined to be equal to the write priority ceiling of O.

Having stated our objectives and our assumptions, we now define the rw_priority ceiling protocol that is used on each processor.

Task τ, having the highest priority among the tasks ready to run, is assigned the processor. Before task τ enters an elementary transaction T, it must first obtain the locks on the data objects that it accesses.

1. Suppose that τ attempts to lock data object O. Let O^* be the data object with the highest rw_priority ceiling of all data objects currently locked by transactions other than those of τ. Task τ will be blocked and the lock on an object O will be denied, if the priority of task τ is not higher than the rw_priority ceiling of data object O^*. In this case, task τ is said to be blocked by the task whose transaction holds the lock on O^*. If task τ's priority is higher than the rw_priority ceiling of O^*, then τ is granted the lock on O[27]. When a task τ exits its elementary transaction, the data objects associated with the transaction will be unlocked.

2. A task τ's transaction T uses its assigned priority, unless it is in its transaction and blocks higher priority transactions. If transaction T blocks higher priority tasks, T *inherits* P_H, the highest priority of the tasks blocked by T. When task τ exits its transaction, it resumes its original priority. Priority inheritance is transitive. Finally, the operations of priority inheritance and of the resumption of original priority must be indivisible.

---

[27]Under this condition, there will be no read-write conflict on the object O, and we need not check if O has been locked.

3. When a task τ does not attempt to enter an elementary transaction, it can preempt another task τ_L executing at a lower priority, inherited or assigned.

Remark: The objective of this protocol is to ensure that each elementary transaction is executed at a higher priority level than the priority levels which can be inherited by preempted elementary transactions. When a task τ write-locks a single object O, the rw_priority ceiling of O represents the highest priority that τ can inherit through O. For example, when τ write-locks O, it can block the highest priority task τ_H that may read or write O and hence inherit τ_H's priority. Therefore, the rw_priority ceiling of a write-locked object is defined to be equal to the absolute priority ceiling. Alternatively, let a low priority task τ hold a read-lock on a data object O and let task τ_w be the highest priority task that may request a write lock on O. Task τ can block τ_w and inherit τ_w's priority. Therefore, the rw_priority ceiling of a read-locked data object is defined as the data object's write priority ceiling. A read-locked object O can be, of course, read-locked again by a task τ_r which has priority higher than that of τ_w. However, in this case, task τ_r has *preempted* τ and there is *no* blocking.

Remark: Under this protocol, we need not explicitly check for the possibility of read-write conflicts. For instance, when an object O is write-locked by a task τ, the rw_priority ceiling is equal to the highest priority task that can access O. Hence, the protocol will block a higher priority task that may want to write or read O. On the other hand, suppose that the object O is read-locked by τ. Then, the rw_priority ceiling of O is equal to the highest priority task that may write O. Hence, a task that attempts to write O will have a priority no higher than the rw_priority ceiling and will be blocked. Only the tasks that read O and have priority higher than the rw_priority ceiling will be allowed to read-lock O, and read-locks are compatible.

Under the rw_priority ceiling protocol, mutual deadlock of transactions cannot occur and each task can be blocked by at most one elementary transaction until it completes or suspends itself. We shall now prove both these properties of the rw_priority ceiling protocol along the same lines as for the priority ceiling protocol in Chapter 2.

Lemma 4-1: Under the rw_priority ceiling protocol, each transaction will execute at a higher priority level than the level that the preempted transactions can inherit.

Proof: By the definition of the rw_priority ceiling protocol, when a task τ locks a set of data objects, the highest priority level τ can inherit is equal to the highest rw_priority ceiling of the data objects locked by τ. Hence, when a task τ_H's priority is higher than the highest rw_priority ceiling of the data objects locked by a transaction **T** of task τ, the transactions of τ_H will execute at a priority that is higher than the preempted transaction **T** can inherit.

Theorem 4-2: There is no mutual deadlock under the rw_priority ceiling protocol.

Proof: Suppose that a mutual deadlock can occur. Let the highest priority of all the tasks involved in the deadlock be P. Due to the transitivity of priority inheritance, all the tasks involved in the deadlock will eventually inherit the same highest priority P. This contradicts Lemma 4-1.

Lemma 4-3: Under the rw_priority ceiling protocol, until task τ either completes its execution or suspends itself, task τ can be blocked at most once by a single elementary transaction of a lower priority task τ_L, even if τ_L has multiple elementary transactions.

Proof: Suppose that task τ is blocked by a lower priority task τ_L. By Theorem 4-2, there will be no deadlock and hence task τ_L will exit its current transaction at some instant t_1. Once task τ_L exits its transaction at time t_1, task τ_L is preempted by τ. Since τ_L is no longer within a transaction, it cannot inherit a higher priority than its own priority unless it enters another transaction. However, τ_L cannot resume execution until τ completes or suspends itself. The Lemma follows.

Theorem 4-4: Under the rw_priority ceiling protocol, a task τ can be blocked by at most a single elementary transaction of one lower priority task until either τ completes its execution or suspends itself.

Proof: Suppose that τ is blocked by n lower priority transactions. By Lemma 4-3, τ must be blocked by the transactions of n different lower priority tasks, $\tau_1, \cdots, \tau_n$, where the priority of τ_i is assumed to be higher than or equal to that of τ_{i+1}. Since a lower priority task cannot block a higher priority task unless it is already in its transaction, tasks $\tau_1, \cdots, \tau_n$ must be in their transactions when τ arrives. By assumption, τ is blocked by τ_n and τ_n inherits the priority of τ. Since τ can be blocked by τ_n, task τ's priority cannot be higher than the highest priority P that can be inherited by τ_n. On the other hand, by lemma 4-1, task τ_{n-1}'s priority is higher than P. It follows that task τ_{n-1}'s priority is higher than that of task τ. This contradicts the assumption that τ's priority is higher than that of tasks $\tau_1, \cdots, \tau_n$.

Corollary 4-5: If a task τ_i suspends itself at most k times, then the above theorem holds with the duration of blocking equal to *k+1* elementary transactions.

<u>Remark:</u> The rw_priority ceiling protocol is selectively restrictive on the sharing of read-locks. The reason is that a direct application of the read and write semantic can lead to prolonged durations of blocking. For example, suppose that we have a single write transaction at the highest priority level and ten lower priority read transactions. If we let ten transactions concurrently holding read-locks on data object **O**, then when a higher priority task arrives later and attempts to write **O**, it has to wait for all ten of these transactions to complete. That is, some forms of concurrency can lengthen the worst-case duration of blocking, resulting in poorer schedulability.

As in Chapter 2, the worst-case blocking duration that each task can encounter can be determined and can be used to check whether a set of periodic tasks with hard deadlines at the end of the periods can be scheduled by the rate-monotonic algorithm [Liu 73] when the rw_priority ceiling protocol is used.

Theorem 4-6: A lower priority write transaction $\mathbf{T_w}$ can block a higher priority task τ with priority P, if and only if $\mathbf{T_w}$ may write-lock a data object whose absolute priority ceiling is higher than or equal to P. A lower priority read transaction $\mathbf{T_r}$ can block a higher priority task τ with priority P, if and only if $\mathbf{T_r}$ may read-lock a data object whose write priority ceiling is higher than or equal to P.

Proof: It directly follows from the definitions of the rw_priority ceiling protocol.

Let Z be the set of elementary transactions that could block task τ. By Theorem 2-12, task τ can be blocked for at most the duration of a single element in Z if it does not suspend itself. Hence the worst-case blocking time for τ is the duration of the longest elementary transaction in Z when τ does not suspend itself. If the task τ suspends itself k times, then the worst-case blocking time is equal to the sum of the *k+1* longest elements in

Z. We denote this worst-case blocking time of task τ_i as B_i. Note that given a set of n periodic tasks, $B_n = 0$, since there is no lower priority task to block τ_n.

In order to test the schedulability of τ_i, we need to consider both the preemptions caused by higher priority tasks and blocking by lower priority tasks along with τ_i's own utilization. The blocking of any instance of τ_i is bounded by B_i. Thus Theorem 2-16, which is repeated here for convenience, applies.

Theorem 4-7: Suppose that a task does not suspend itself from initiation to completion. A set of n periodic tasks can be scheduled by the rate monotonic algorithm if the following conditions are satisfied:

$$\forall\, i,\, 1 \le i \le n,\ \frac{C_1}{T_1} + \frac{C_2}{T_2} + \cdots + \frac{C_i}{T_i} + \frac{B_i}{T_i} \le i(2^{1/i} - 1)$$

4.2.3. Extending the rw_Priority Ceiling Protocol

The underlying principle of the rw_priority ceiling protocol is that the effective ceiling of a locked resource is the priority of the highest priority task that can no longer use the resource in that state. If the type of locking is such that the resource can no longer be used by some requests, the ceiling is set to the highest priority of these conflicting requests. Once the ceiling of locked resources is set in this fashion, a future request is honored only if it has a higher priority than the highest priority ceiling of locked resources. When this locking protocol is used, a higher priority task would still be blocked for at most the duration of a single critical section of a lower priority task. In addition, mutual deadlock would be avoided.

This principle can be used to extend the rw_priority ceiling protocol to solve other related problems. For instance, it can be extended to act as an effective priority ceiling protocol when there are multiple instances of a given resource and more than one instance of the resource can be requested at a time by a task [Baker 90]. A resource's absolute priority ceiling is the ceiling of the highest priority task that can request instances of this resource. The effective ceiling (similar to the rw_priority ceiling) of the resource depends upon the number of instances n of the resource that remain. The effective ceiling is the priority of the highest priority task that would submit a request for more than n remaining instances of the resource. Whenever a request for m instances of a resource is received from a job J, the resource allocation is made only if J's priority is higher than the highest effective priority ceiling of any resource that has already been allocated.

The read-write semantics of locks was chosen merely as an example of some locks being shareable and others not. This can be extended to include other types of locks such as the modified readers-writers problem where only write-locks conflict and readers can share the lock with a single writer[28]. In this case, when a data object is unlocked or read-locked, its rw_ceiling is set to 0. When the object is write-locked, the rw_ceiling is set to the priority of the highest priority writer which can write that object. As a result, any reader with higher priority than the highest priority writer can still share the lock with a current writer. If an object is read-locked, any reader or the first writer can still share the lock.

4.3 DISTRIBUTED DATABASE ISSUES

In this section, we investigate the use of rw_priority ceiling protocol as a basis for real-time concurrency control in a distributed environment. While a locking protocol is still an efficient method to ensure consistency within a node, holding locks across the network is unattractive. Owing to communication delay, locking across the network will only force the local copy to be as outdated as the remote copies and this is counter-productive for real-time applications such as tracking. It is better to have an up-to-date local copy and let the remote copies be historical versions. That is, we will adopt a multiple version approach for concurrency control for distributed data objects. The priority driven and locking based concurrency control protocol will be used within each node in the the network. In addition, we assume a single writer and multiple readers model for distributed data objects. This is a simple model that effectively models applications such as distributed tracking in which each radar station main-

---

[28]One instance of this problem arises in the run-time monitoring of system invariants that must be maintained by tasks [Chodrow 91].

tains its view and makes it available to other nodes in the network. The extension to multiple writers is presented at the end of this section.

In a distributed database environment, an atomic data set is a logical unit of data objects for distribution, because it represents a logically consistent view. An elementary transaction operating upon an ADS represents an atomic unit of operation for concurrent execution. For example, a global ADS G can be the union of many local track ADS's and a global track ADS. Each ADS in the union can reside on a different computer. To address the problem of reliability, we can replicate an atomic data set on another processor. It may seem that the replicated ADS and the original ADS are part of a single atomic data set; however, they are *two* atomic data sets if one is allowed to be a historical version of the other [Sha 88]. For example, suppose that we have two ADS's residing on two nodes in a network: $A_1 = \{O_1\}$ and its copy $A_2 = \{O_2\}$. If we insist that A_1 and A_2 must be identical with respect to all references, i.e. $O_1 = O_2$, then these data objects will be part of a single ADS. The updates to them must appear to be an instantaneous event with respect to other transactions that access O_1 and O_2. This can be accomplished by using the setwise two-phase locking protocol to perform synchronous updates to O_1 and O_2. However, locking them across the network can lead to long durations of blocking, because of the communication delay. To satisfy the requirement of one being a historical copy of the other, A_1 and A_2 can be modeled as two ADS's and be updated asynchronously. The following is the pseudo-code of the compound transaction Update_Both that maintains a historical relationship between A_1 and A_2. Note that there is no attempt to ensure that other transactions will read identical versions of O_1 and O_2.

```
Compound_Transaction Update_Both;
BeginParallel
   Elementary_Transaction Update_Local_Copy_A₁
   BeginSerial
      Lock O₁
      O₁ = new_value;
      Unlock O₁
   EndSerial;

   Elementary_Transaction Update_Remote_Copy_A₂
   BeginSerial
      Lock O₂
      O₂ = new_value;
      Unlock O₂
   EndSerial;
EndParallel;
```

While atomic data sets provide us with logically consistent views, the copies of the logically consistent views could be, owing to the delays in the network, temporally inconsistent. That is, some of the views can be out of date. There are applications where a *temporally* consistent view is better than just the latest information that can be obtained at each site. In an application like tracking, a local track would be updated periodically in conjunction with repetitive scans. Hence, in order to provide a temporal consistency in a distributed environment, we can utilize the periodicity of the writer as a timestamp mechanism. For example, given an ADS and its replication, if for each data object there is only a single periodic writer and if the deadlines of this single periodic writer can be guaranteed on all the processors, then all these data objects will be updated by the end of the writer's period. That is, on each processor, during period n the versions of period $(n-1)$ are consistent. It is, of course, difficult to observe identical deadlines on local and remote processors because of the network communication delay. Typically, the versions of the data objects at remote sites will lag behind the local site. Thus, the problem of ensuring a temporally consistent view becomes a network-level real-time scheduling problem in which the time lags in the distributed versions are controlled. Once the lags are controlled, distributed tasks can read the proper versions of the distributed data objects and ensure that their decisions are based upon temporally consistent data. When all the tasks in each scheduling element in the network, e.g. processor or communication medium, are scheduled by the rate-monotonic algorithm, the version lag between two replicated data objects in a network is bounded by the number of scheduling elements on its update path.

Lemma 4-8: Let $A_i[v]$ denote the version v of an ADS residing in processor i. Suppose that ADS A_1 and its replications, $\{A_1, \cdots, A_n\}$, are distributed in n processors. Assume that a real-time scheduling algorithm guarantees that $max(v_i, v_j) \leq k$, $1 \leq i, j \leq n$. That is, the maximal lag between the versions of these ADS's at different processors is bounded by k. At period n, we have $\{A_1[n-k] = A_2[n-k] = \cdots = A_m[n-k]$, $n \geq k\}$ available at all the n processors.

Proof: The Lemma follows directly from our single writer assumption and our assumption that the maximal lag is k.

Remark: Since we do not have deadlock within each processor and locks are not allowed to be held across processor boundaries, we do not have the problem of distributed deadlocks.

To calculate the version lags, each scheduling element on the path is counted as a node. Thus, if two replicated data objects reside in two processors connected by a communication medium, we consider that there are three nodes on the path: the local processor, the communication medium and the remote processor. For example, suppose that we have a set of processors connected by a communication bus and that all the processors and communication bus are scheduled by the rate monotonic algorithm.[29] Let ADS A_1 and A_2 reside in two different processors and A_1 be at the home site. The rate monotonic algorithm guarantees that A_1 can be updated by the end of the first period. That is, we can initiate the *send* operation no later than the starting time of the second period. The rate monotonic algorithm on the communication medium ensures that the message will be delivered to the receiving processor by the end of the second period. It follows that the "update A_2" request is ready at the initiation time of the third period and can be carried out by the end of the third period.

Theorem 4-9: When all the tasks in every element of the network are schedulable by the rate-monotonic algorithm, the ver-

---

[29]Readers who are interested in the scheduling issues of communication media are referred to [Lehoczky 86a].

sion lag between two replicated ADS's in a network is bounded by the number of nodes on its update path.

Proof: Suppose that replicated ADS's A_1 and A_2 can be updated within the same period. The version lag is 1, because ADS A_1 can be updated before A_2. But both of them will be updated by the end of the same period. Thus, the lag between the versions of these two ADS's is at most 1. By introducing each additional full period delay between the updates of the two ADS's, the version lag increases by 1. That is, when the updates are separated by n periods, the version lag is at most $(n + 1)$. When there are k nodes on the path, A_1 will be updated by the end of the first period and A_2 will be updated by the end of the kth period. That is, they are separated by at most $(k-1)$ periods. It follows that the version lag between them is at most $(k-1) + 1 = k$.

Corollary 4-10: When all the tasks in every element of the network are schedulable by the rate-monotonic algorithm, the time lag between the information provided by two replicated ADS's in a network is bounded by the product of the writer period and the number of nodes on its update path.

Remark: This approach can be extended to address the multiple readers and writers problem when a home site of an ADS can be defined. We first require all the writers to write the ADS at the home site by following the setwise two-phase locking protocol with rw_priority ceiling. This ensures the logical consistency of the ADS at the home site. For remote copies of this ADS, we can let the highest frequency writer τ_H to copy the home site ADS versions over to the remote sites. For example, suppose that the latest update to ADS A by τ_H produces $A[5]$ and the next update of A by τ_H produces $A[7]$, i.e., some other transaction updated A once during the interval between τ_H's updates. In this case, τ will copy over both $A[6]$ and $A[7]$ to the remote sites. The time lag for the information between the home site and remote sites is given by Corollary 4-10. Since τ_H writes all the sites periodically, a logically and temporally consistent view can be obtained by reading the properly delayed versions produced by τ_H.

4.4 SUMMARY

Distributed real-time database is an important area of research with applications ranging from surveillance to reliable manufacturing and production control. A concurrency control theory is normally used to ensure that the integrity and consistency of data in the database(s), and a higher concurrency in accessing the database is considered desirable in general. However, the sharing of read-locks on a uniprocessor is beneficial in real-time systems only when the readers have higher priority than the highest priority writer. Else, the duration of priority inversion can unnecessarily increase. Thus, compatible locks are not necessarily useful in real-time systems, and need to be exploited only when they enhance guaranteed real-time performance. The read-write priority ceiling protocol achieves exactly this effect. It is also possible to extend the read-write priority ceiling protocol to related problems such as allocating multiple instances of a resource, and other types of compatible locks.

The setwise two-phase locking protocol, a modular concurrency control theory, assumes that the database can be decomposed into atomic data sets (ADS's), the consistency of each of which can be maintained independent of the others. It is possible to integrate this setwise two-phase locking protocol, with the read-write priority ceiling protocol, which in turn is a real-time scheduling protocol. The result is the creation of a real-time database concurrency control protocol. This integrated approach is free from deadlocks and bounds the priority inversion encountered by a task at each processor to the duration of at most one elementary transaction until it suspends itself or completes. In addition, the schedulability analysis of a set of periodic tasks with embedded transactions becomes possible. Finally, assuming that each ADS is bound to a single processor, a logically and temporally consistent view can be provided in a distributed environment, where multiple versions of data with different ages are provided to users.

Chapter Five

Conclusion

Real-time systems are of immense practical significance. These systems are used to control, monitor or perform critical operations and to respond quickly to emergency events in a wide range of civilian and military settings. These systems must often function in an environment which does not permit human interaction with the system or operate on a time-scale which is too short for effective human interaction and intervention. Real-time systems are required to process tasks that have stringent timing requirements, and they must perform these tasks in a way that these timing requirements are guaranteed to be met. Nevertheless, the scientific foundations underlying the practice of determining the ability of a particular system to meet its timing requirements are limited. Many of the limitations of this scientific theory arise because the theory is typically based on idealized assumptions and does not take into account the realities that are encountered in actual systems.

Prioritized preemptive scheduling is a methodology that has been studied fairly extensively in the literature. Scheduling algorithms such as the rate-monotonic, earliest deadline, value function and least slack-time algorithms have been proposed, and their properties analyzed. As a consequence, the use of these algorithms can help to base the development of real-time systems on a scientific platform. This would be in direct contrast to the use of *ad hoc* techniques like the use of cyclical executives (alias execution time-lines), which are highly brittle in nature. Analytical techniques can eliminate this inflexible design approach, and lead to considerable benefits in terms of reduced software development, maintenance and modification costs. However, before these techniques can be used in practice, realistic factors such as synchronization and data-sharing must be taken into account. In particular, the following approximation of the idealized model of priority driven preemptive scheduling is required.

- The resource allocation must be consistent with the priority ordering of tasks.

- The duration of blocking due to synchronization and mutual exclusion requirements should not be a function of non-critical section execution times.
- The preemption cost must be small relative to task timing constraints.

That is, as preemptive cost and critical section duration approach zero, we must tend towards an idealized environment. This book focuses upon and achieves the first two objectives.

5.1 SUMMARY OF RESULTS

Much of the scheduling work in the literature assumes that tasks are independent of one another and do not share any resources. However, in reality, the sharing of logical and/or physical resources is inevitable, and the problem of synchronization needs to be addressed. An indiscriminate use of existing synchronization primitives can, unfortunately, lead to unbounded priority inversion, where a high priority task can be blocked by lower priority tasks for an arbitrarily long duration of time. While priority inversion cannot be totally eliminated from a system, it is essential that the duration of priority inversion be bounded and, if possible, minimized such that the penalty due to priority inversion is tolerable, or even negligible. Only then can prioritized preemptive scheduling techniques be used to build real-time systems with predictable timing behavior.

Chapter 2 presents the concept of priority inheritance, by which a job blocking higher priority jobs inherits the priority of the highest priority job that it blocks. This concept of priority inheritance can be used to solve the unbounded priority inversion problem. An entire family of protocols are developed based on priority inheritance which, in addition, minimize the duration of priority inversion that a task can encounter. The basic priority inheritance protocol solves the unbounded priority inversion problem, but is still faced with two problems. Mutual deadlocks can occur, and a task can still be blocked for a long duration of time. The priority ceiling protocol allows resources to be allocated selectively, thereby avoiding deadlocks and ensuring that a job can encounter priority inversion for no more than the duration of a single critical section. Nevertheless, the priority ceiling protocol is unnecessarily restrictive in that it disallows some resource allocations from being made. The semaphore control protocol is an optimal priority inheritance protocol in the sense that it embeds necessary and sufficient conditions for a resource to be allocated but still achieve the two desirable properties of the priority ceiling protocol. This protocol is also optimal in the sense that no other priority inheritance protocol can guarantee a better worst-case duration of priority inversion for a job. The resulting bounded duration of priority inversion can be used to carry out the schedulability analysis for a given task set using these protocols.

Chapter 2 also demonstrates that the priority inheritance protocols can be simply and efficiently implemented. An efficient implementation strategy for the priority ceiling protocol, which eliminates semaphore queues, is presented. Under this implementation, jobs that block due to these protocols need not be removed from the ready job queue. The basic inheritance protocol and priority ceiling protocol have also been implemented in an Ada run-time system. Experiments using a simulator and an Ada run-time system show that the priority inheritance protocols provide better guaranteed and actual performance under a wide range of situations, in avoiding deadlocks and under transient overload conditions.

Chapter 3 addresses the problem of unbounded waiting time for access to global resources in multiple processor systems. The availability of multiprocessors has expanded greatly, and is expected to grow even more due to the expected slowdown in the rate of increase of uniprocessor speeds. The potential speedup of applications has motivated this use of multiprocessors, and they are finding wider use in real-time systems as well. The priority inversion problem, as can be expected, becomes worse in the context of multiple processor systems, and the priority ceiling protocol needs to be extended to multiple processor systems. The distributed priority ceiling protocol prevents deadlocks, and bounds the duration that a task has to wait for access to global data and/or resources. These properties allow us to derive a set of sufficient conditions to check whether a given task set can satisfy its timing constraints. This protocol is well suited to distributed systems using remote procedure calls for interprocessor resource sharing. We also define a variation called the shared memory priority ceiling protocol that can be implemented more efficiently on shared memory multiprocessors. Appropriate task allocation schemes must be used to bind tasks to processors.

Chapter 4 studies the real-time synchronization problem in the context of distributed real-time databases. In particular, the interplay between a concurrency control theory and the real-time synchronization protocols is investigated. Distributed real-time databases are used in many applications ranging from surveillance to reliable manufacturing. Some kind of concurrency control theory such as two-phase locking, or tree-based locking is typically employed to ensure the integrity and consistency of data residing in the database. In general, a protocol that allows more concurrency in accessing a database is considered more desirable. However, in the context of real-time systems, higher concurrency does not necessarily mean better performance. In particular, the sharing of read-locks is beneficial only when the readers of a data object have higher priority than the highest priority writer of the data object. The duration of priority inversion encountered by a transaction can increase otherwise. The read-write priority ceiling protocol is designed to exploit the semantics of compatible locks only when it enhances guaranteed real-time performance. This read-write protocol can be integrated with concurrency control protocols, such as the setwise two-phase locking protocol to create a real-time database concurrency control protocol. This integrated protocol frees the system from mutual deadlocks, and again bounds the duration of priority inversion encountered by a task to at most the duration of one elementary transaction. The scheme can be extended to provide a logically and temporally consistent view in a distributed environment, where multiple versions of data with different ages are available to users. It is also possible to extend the read-write priority ceiling protocol to related problems such as allocating multiple instances of a resource, and other types of compatible locks.

In summary, the previous chapters address the unpredictable timing problem arising from the direct use of existing synchronization primitives, and develop synchronization protocols for use on uniprocessors, multiple processor systems and decomposable distributed real-time databases. These protocols bound the time that a task has to wait for a lower priority task to access a shared resource. This results in an environment close to the idealized environment, and the schedulability loss for a task set due to resource sharing turns out to be relatively small on uniprocessors and acceptable in multiple processor systems.

5.2 DIRECTIONS FOR FUTURE RESEARCH

The protocols presented in this book offer two complementary benefits. First, they solve the priority inversion problem on uniprocessors and real-time databases and address remote blocking problems in multiple processor systems. At the same time, these protocols fit well within the rate-monotonic framework. As such, further research that can be done to advance our work can be classified into two categories: theoretical solutions to newer problems within the rate-monotonic and related frameworks, and the implementation and evaluation of some protocols which were developed as part of this research. We discuss below some potential future directions for research.

Scheduling theory for real-time systems in general assume that the underlying hardware and the software on it do not fail. However, in many critical systems, fault-tolerance requirements can be as important as the predictable timing behavior of the system. For example, the timing constraints would no longer be guaranteed if the results from a remote procedure call are not received. Traditional approaches to fault-tolerance employ some form of temporal and/or spatial redundancy to combat the impact of unreliable components. However, in real-time systems, spatial redundancy can be relatively costly due to power and volume constraints, whereas tight timing constraints can limit the flexibility of temporal redundancy. Newer approaches or intelligent compromises may be necessary to obtain the benefits of predictability and fault-tolerance. The integration of fault-tolerance with scheduling approaches is a widely open research domain, and the effect of faults on system temporal behavior needs to be better understood.

A functional requirement for a system can be that a signal must be sampled, processed, and displayed within a certain time interval. However, the signal may pass through several processing elements. For instance, the sampling can be done by a dedicated interrupt processor, processed by one or more special-purpose and/or general-purpose processors, and processed for display on another console processor. Hence, the actual deadline for this activity is on the entire task, and not on individual subtasks. This problem is referred to as the *end-to-end* scheduling problem, which remains unsolved for the general case.

The read-write priority ceiling protocol is applicable to distributed real-time databases, if the database can be decomposed such that locks on objects need not be held across processor boundaries. For example, if the setwise two-phase locking protocol is used, the database should be decomposed into multiple atomic data sets such that each ADS can be bound to a single processor. However, there exist applications where locks on objects have to be held across processors. This generalized real-time database problem is still open.

The multiprocessor priority ceiling protocol assumes that the network communication overhead is negligible, which is not necessarily the case. When the communication medium connecting the processors is sufficiently loaded, the messages between processors must be scheduled as well. While scheduling algorithms exist for backplanes and token-rings, the scheduling of the processors and the network needs to be integrated. This problem might perhaps also be construed as a variation of the end-to-end scheduling problem.

The protocols developed in this book use semaphores primarily as locking mechanisms. However, semaphores can be used for other paradigms such as the producer-consumer model. While some work has been done in this area, the results and possible approaches are not as well understood.

The distributed priority ceiling protocol has been defined both in terms of semaphores and under the semantics of Ada. The latter fits well within the virtual node concept being proposed for the distribution semantics of Ada [Wellings 88]. The implementation of the protocol is also fairly simple since the priority ceiling protocol can be implemented easily and efficiently, and the distributed protocol merely runs the priority ceiling protocol locally on each of the processors. However, an implementation and evaluation of this protocol and its variation, the multiprocessor priority ceiling protocol, has been outside the scope of this book. The actual performance of these protocols needs to be studied.

The read_write priority ceiling protocol for real-time databases exploits compatible locks only when they enhance guaranteed system performance. The University of Virginia's database prototyping tool [Son 88] has been used at the University to compare the performance of the rw_priority ceiling protocol against two phase locking with and without priority assignments to tasks. This experiment investigated performance characteristics in a single site database system. They show that the read_write priority ceiling protocol does, indeed, provide better performance. However, their studies considered only single-shot transactions on a single-site database. The read_write ceiling protocol needs to be implemented and evaluated in the context of multiple database sites and for periodic transactions.

5.3 CONCLUDING REMARKS

The area of real-time system design is a very rich domain for research problems spanning multiple spheres of expertise in computer science and engineering. At a high level of abstraction, a well-defined methodology based on sound mathematical foundations must be adopted for the behavior of the real-time system to be easily understood and modified. Else, the woes of inflexibility and hand-crafting that have plagued real-time system design over the years will continue to dominate, escalating the life-cycle costs of present and future real-time systems of large complexity. Examples of such systems might include fully automated manufacturing and quality control operations, intelligent nation-wide power stations and grids, space stations, manned space missions, and sophisticated defense systems.

To achieve the goals of such a scientific methodology, all layers of the system right from the system-level functional requirements, across the software layers including the run-time system and the application, down to the hardware architecture on which the software executes must be designed and developed with the same methodology in mind. In other words, layers designed with one application in mind (say hardware components designed for commercial data-processing) should not be forced to be used in a real-time system, where the figures of merit are entirely different and sometimes even the opposite of those in commercial non-real-time applications. For example, the Ethernet protocol for LAN traffic does not suit real-time requirements: it introduces unpredictable communication timing behavior, and its performance downgrades with higher loads. Even current advances in the implementation of computer architectures run against the special requirements of real-time systems. For a real-time system to provide *a priori* guaranteed performance, it must be possible to bound and predict the time that it takes to execute a segment of code. However, techniques like on-chip caches, extensive pipelining and prefetching, and multiple register sets can cause even the same piece of code to consume different time-intervals depending upon the time and possibly nested procedure level at which it is executed. This introduces unpredictability at the lowest level of the hardware, and the requirement to build a predictable real-time system on top of such hardware either cannot be met, or very pessimistic worst-case assumptions must be made.

In the domain of scheduling, algorithms need to be developed to schedule real-time tasks at high levels of processor utilization, and their properties formally analyzed and proved. In order for these algorithms to be of practical use, "reality factors" such as task synchronization, context switching overhead, aperiodic tasks, jitter, mode changes etc. must be considered. These algorithms must then be coded at an appropriate level of abstraction, necessitating the availability of a programming language with a flexible set of semantically rich primitives. Compile-time support must also be available to optimize a given embedded application such that maximum performance is extracted without the overhead of supporting options which seldom get exercised. Finally, the hardware architecture must facilitate and not impede the implementation of the scheduling and programming paradigms.

The harnessing of the complexity of tomorrow's real-time systems poses a formidable challenge. Furthermore, ever-increasing hardware capabilities bring to the domain of real-time systems problems that were not previously considered solvable in real-time. For example, highly dynamic real-time AI problems are being defined, and dependable real-time embedded systems that will function for several years continuously without human interference are being contemplated. In order to meet these (apparently futuristic) goals, advances in software engineering techniques must be accompanied by large strides in the understanding of designing real-time systems. The significance of the software engineering domain is being steadily recognized, but the emphasis on understanding and improving the technology for real-time systems needs to increase many-fold. Hopefully, this book is a positive step in this direction.

Appendix A

Computing B_i For The Basic Inheritance Protocol

In this appendix, we present a branch-and-bound search technique to find the upper-bound on the blocking delay for each task when the basic priority inheritance protocol is used.

Under the basic priority inheritance protocol, a task τ_i can be blocked by a lower priority task τ_L if τ_L locks a semaphore S that is also locked by a task with a priority equal to or greater than that of τ_i. Similarly, a task τ_i can be blocked by a semaphore S if S can be locked by a task with lower priority than τ_i and a task with equal or greater priority. From Theorems 2-3 and 2-6, a lower priority task can block τ_i for a maximum of a single critical section while a semaphore S can block τ_i for a maximum of a single critical section. Thus, if there are n lower priority tasks that can block τ_i and m semaphores that can block τ_i, the worst-case blocking duration of τ_i is the duration of at most $\min(m,n)$ critical sections. We still need to determine the worst-case blocking duration and carry it out as follows.

We denote the maximum duration that a task τ_i needs to lock a semaphore S_j as $\delta_{i,j}$. The maximum duration is applicable because a task may access the same semaphore several times and the maximum blocking delay would correspond to this maximum duration.

Let us assume that we need to find the upper-bound of the blocking delay for task τ_i. Consider each task τ_j that has lower priority than τ_i and that accesses semaphores which are also accessed by τ_i or higher priority tasks. Build a one-level tree for each τ_i-τ_j pair with each edge representing a semaphore S_k that is shared with τ_i or a higher priority task. The weight of each edge is $\delta_{j,k}$, the maximum duration of any access to this semaphore by τ_j.

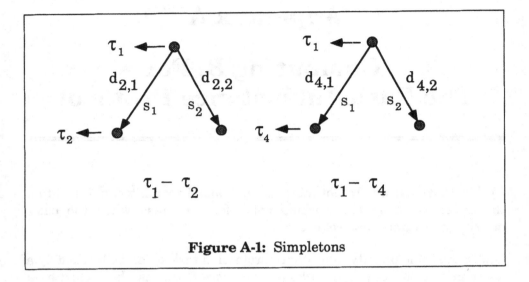

Figure A-1: Simpletons

We first describe our approach using an example. Consider a task set $\{(\tau_1, \{S_1, S_2\}), (\tau_2, \{S_1, S_2\}), (\tau_3, \{\}), (\tau_4, \{S_1, S_2\})\}$, i.e. tasks τ_1, τ_2 and τ_4 need to access S_1, and S_2 during execution and τ_3 does not access any semaphores. We assume rate-monotonic priority assignment is in effect and let priority(τ_1) > priority(τ_2) > priority(τ_3) > priority(τ_4).

Let the maximum durations that τ_2 needs to lock S_1 and S_2 be $\delta_{2,1}$ and $\delta_{2,2}$ respectively and the maximum durations that τ_4 will lock S_1 and S_2 be $\delta_{4,1}$ and $\delta_{4,2}$ respectively.

Suppose τ_1 is the task whose blocking delay is to be found. Then, the two trees corresponding to the τ_1-τ_2 and τ_1-τ_4 pairs will be as shown in Figure A-1. The pair τ_1-τ_3 need not be considered since τ_3 does not share any semaphores with τ_1 (or higher priority tasks of which there are none now). We refer to these one-level trees as *simpletons*.

The final search tree for τ_i would be built in multiple steps.

1. Pick any simpleton and make it the first level of the tree. The simpleton corresponding to the τ_i-τ_k pair where $k=min$(all possible j's) is a good choice.

2. Pick any unused simpleton and attach it to *each* of the leaves from the previous step. Again, the simpleton corresponding to the τ_i-τ_k pair where $k=min$(unused j's) is a good choice.

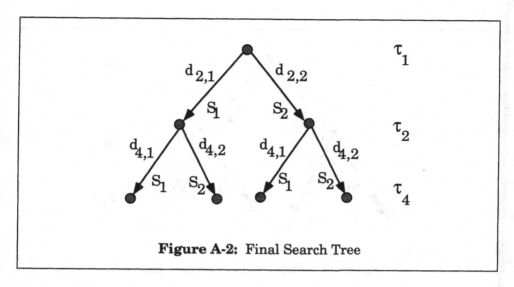

Figure A-2: Final Search Tree

3. Repeat step 2 until all simpletons are used up.

The final search tree for the above example is shown in figure A-2.

The problem of finding the exact bounding delay now becomes one of finding the maximum weight of a path from the root to one of the leaves. The weight of the path, however, is *not* necessarily the sum of the weights on the edges along the path. The weight of an edge contributes to the path weight only under two conditions:

1. The semaphore corresponding to this edge has not been encountered along this path. In this case, the weight of the edge is added to the weight of the path.

2. If the semaphore has already been encountered along the path, the weight of this edge is considered only if the weight corresponding to the already encountered semaphore is less than the weight of this edge. If this is the case, the weight that is added to the path weight is only the difference between the weights of the present edge and the already encountered edge.

In order to avoid confusion, we refer to this modified weight of a path as its *transformed weight*. The transformed weight of a path from the root to a node is called the value of the node. The computation of the maximum transformed weight of a path for the above example is shown in figure A-3.

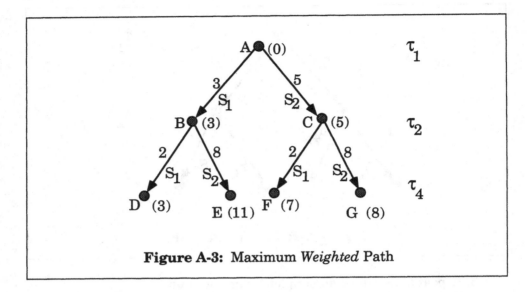

Figure A-3: Maximum *Weighted* Path

Let $\delta_{2,1} = 3$, $\delta_{2,2} = 5$, $\delta_{4,1} = 2$, and $\delta_{4,2} = 8$. The root (node A) has value 0. Perform a pre-order traversal of the tree. Initially when we reach node B, B takes the value 3 and the only semaphore encountered so far is S_1. Next, the edge BD represents the semaphore S_1 and since it has already been encountered, and the present weight of 2 is less than the previously encountered weight for S_1 (3), node D also gets the value 3. Then, since the edge BE represents S_2 which has not been encountered, node E takes the value (3 + 8) 11. We next reach node C which takes the value 5 and the semaphore encountered is S_2. Edge CF represents S_1 and hence E takes the value (5 + 2) 7. However, edge CG represents S_2 which has been encountered at AC. Since weight(CG) > weight(AC), node G takes the value (5 − 5 + 8) 8 and the traversal is complete. The path with the maximum transformed weight is found to be ABE and hence, β_1 is given by 11.

While the worst-case situation for this tree search can correspond to an exhaustive search, it is possible to prune the construction of the tree using branch-and-bound techniques. At any node in the tree, there exists an upper bound to the maximum weight to a path that is possible from this node and is given by the value of the node and the sum of the maximum possible weight at each level of the tree. This bound can be used to prune the search, which proceeds as follows.

Perform a pre-order traversal of the tree assigning values to nodes. The

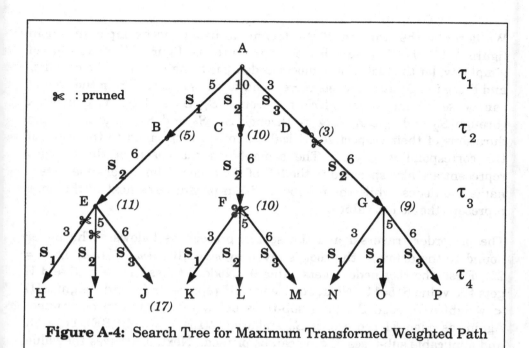

Figure A-4: Search Tree for Maximum Transformed Weighted Path

values represent the transformed weight of the path from the root to this node. When a path has been found to a leaf and its transformed weight is largest of those seen so far, remember this weight. The following two rules can then be used to prune the tree search.

- *Rule 1*: At any node, compute the upper bound of the transformed weight of any path that is possible from this node. This is done by adding to the value of the node the maximum weight possible at each level below this node. If this upper bound is less than the maximum transformed weight of a path found so far, the sub-tree below this node can be pruned.

- *Rule 2*: Consider a node with a branching factor of n. If any of these n edges corresponds to an already encountered semaphore in the path to this node and its weight is less than the previously encountered weight (i.e. the weight of this edge will not be added to the transformed weight of this path), the sub-tree from this edge can be pruned. However, if $n-1$ edges have been pruned from this node, the nth edge and the subtree below it *must* be considered regardless of the edge's weight and the semaphore that it corresponds to.

We describe the working of the technique using the example shown in figure A-4. The final search tree is given in the figure. For the sake of simplicity, let the task whose blocking delay is being measured be called τ_1 and those in successive levels correspond to τ_2, τ_3 and τ_4. From the tree, it can be seen that τ_2 can block τ_1 through S_1, S_2 and S_3, τ_3 can block through S_2 and τ_4 can block τ_1 through S_1, S_2 and S_3. The maximum durations of their respective critical sections are specified to the right of the corresponding edges. The semaphores that each of these edges represent are also specified to the left of the edges. The upper-case letters name the nodes, while the numbers within parantheses next to the node represent the nodes' values.

The pre-order traversal and the search proceed as follows. The upper bound to the delay at the root is given by $max(5,10,3)+max(6)+max(3,5,6) = 22$. First, the root node A gets value 0. Node B takes the value 5 and E gets the value 6+5=11. Next, since edge EH represents S_1 and weight(EH) < weight(AB), edge EH (and sub-trees below it, if any) can be pruned. Again, as edge EI represents S_2 and weight(EI) < weight(BE), edge EI and applicable sub-trees, if any, can be pruned. Next, J receives the value 11+6=17. Since this completes a path from the root to a leaf and is the maximum so far, we remember it.

The traversal takes us next to C which receives the value 10. At F, we compute the upper bound of paths from C and find it to be 10+6+6=22. Since this is greater than the maximum weight of 17 we have found so far, we proceed to F. Now, since CF represents S_2 and weight(CF) < weight(AC), the edge and the sub-tree below it would be pruned. However, since this is the only child edge at node C, from rule 2, the sub-tree cannot be pruned and the search continues with F taking the value 10. We now compute the upper bound of a path from node F. Since the maximum possible weight below C is 6, the upper bound is given by 10+6=16. This weight is less than the maximum weight of 17 already found and hence the entire sub-tree below F can be pruned.

We move on to node D which gets the value 3. We now compute the upper bound for paths from D. We find it to be 3+6+6=15. As this upper bound is less than the maximum weight already found, we prune the entire sub-tree below D. This completes our traversal and the blocking delay for τ_1 corresponds to the maximum weight of 17.

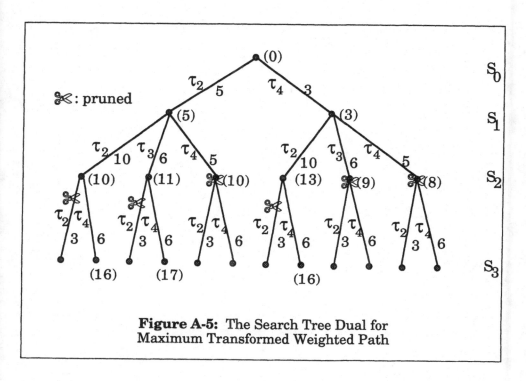

Figure A-5: The Search Tree Dual for
Maximum Transformed Weighted Path

The need for the exception case in rule 2 is demonstrated by the need to consider the sub-tree below C if AC has a weight of, say, 12. In this case, the maximum weighted path corresponds to ACFM and the blocking delay is 18.

An alternative representation of the same problem is also possible. Instead of a simpleton's edges representing semaphores and nodes representing tasks, its dual in which nodes represent semaphores and edges represent tasks can also be constructed. We present one such *dual search tree* corresponding to the search tree of Figure A-4 in Figure A-5. The weights are "transformed" if the same task repeats along a path. The sub-trees that are pruned and the nodes whose values would be computed using the same technique as before are also illustrated. The maximum blocking delay is again found to be 17.

Other optimizations are also possible by rearranging the order of the semaphores and/or tasks.

Appendix B

Notation Used

We list the notation used in this book below.

General Notation

J_i A job. Each job is a sequence of instructions that will continuously use the processor until its completion if it is executing alone on the processor. Jobs do not suspend, say, for I/O operations. If they do, they can be accommodated by defining two or more jobs.

τ_i A task. A task represents a job that recurs over time. For example, a *periodic task* is a sequence of the same type of job occurring at regular intervals, and an *aperiodic task* is a sequence of the same type of job occurring at irregular intervals.

C_i The worst-case execution time of job J_i.

T_i The period of a periodic task τ_i.

U_i The utilization of periodic task $\tau_i = C_i/T_i$.

U The total utilization of a periodic task set $= \sum_{i=1}^{n} \frac{C_i}{T_i}$.

B_i The maximum duration that a job J_i of a task τ_i can be blocked (does not include preemption times by a higher priority task).

S_i A binary semaphore guarding a shared data or resource.

$z_{i,j,k}$ The kth critical section in job J_i guarded by S_j.

$P()$	The **P** operation on a semaphore.
$V()$	The **V** operation on a semaphore.
P_i	The priority of job $J_i = p(J_i)$.
$p(J_i)$	The priority of job $J_i = P_i$.
$c(S)$	The priority ceiling of semaphore S. This is defined as the priority of the highest priority job which can request S.
$\beta_{i,j}$	The set of all critical sections of a lower priority job J_j which can block J_i.
$\beta_{i,j}^*$	The set of maximal elements of $\beta_{i,j}$. In other words, it contains the longest critical sections of J_j which can block J_i and eliminates redundant inner critical sections.
β^*	The set of all longest critical sections that can block J_i.
S^*	When J requests S, this is the semaphore with the highest priority ceiling locked by jobs other than J. S^* is not unique under the semaphore control protocol.
J^*	The job holding the lock on S^*.

Semaphore Control Protocol

SL^*	The set of semaphores already locked by the current critical section of J^*.
SR^*	The set of semaphores that will be locked by the current critical section of J^*.
SR	The set of semaphores that the current critical section of J will lock later.

Multiple Processor Systems

P_G	The base priority ceiling for global semaphores (usually defined as $p(J_1)+1$.

gcs A global critical section for a semaphore accessed by tasks bound to two or more processors.

lcs A local critical section accessed only tasks bound to the same processor.

$\wp_i$ A processor in a multiple processor system.

$\wp_{G_j}$ A synchronization processor which executes gcs's. Can also execute non-gcs code.

n_i^G The number of (outermost) gcs's that J_i executes before its completion.

CS_i The total duration that a job J_i spends within gcs's, when executing alone on synchronization processors.

$n_{i,j}^G$ The number of (outermost) gcs's on processor $\wp_{G_j}$ that a job J_i enters before its completion.

$CS_{i,j}$ The total duration that a job J_i spends within gcs's on $\wp_{G_j}$, when executing alone on the synchronization processor.

$C_{non\text{-}cs}$ The computation time of a task outside all critical sections.

C_{lcs} The computation time of a task within critical sections guarded by local semaphores only.

C_{gcs} The computation time of a task within critical sections guarded by global semaphores only.

C_{local} The computation time of a task within its host processor excluding execution times on remote synchronization processors.

U_{local} The utilization of a task on its local processor given by $C_{local}/$Period.

$\{G_i\}$ The set of global server tasks whose services are required by τ_i.

$\wp_r$ A blocking processor for a task τ_i. A gcs on $\wp_r$ is assigned a higher priority than another gcs z on $\wp_r$ guarded by S_G, and τ_i locks S_G.

$NL_{i,j}$ The number of jobs with lower priority than J_i on processor $\wp_j$.

$\{J'_{i,r}\}$ The set of jobs on J_i's blocking processor $\wp_r$ with gcs's having higher priority than gcs's which can directly block J_i.

$NH_{i,r,k}$ The number of gcs's of a job $J_k \in \{J'_{i,r}\}$ with higher priority than a gcs on $\wp_r$ which can directly block J_i.

$\{GS_{i,k}\}$ The set of global semaphores each of which will be locked by both jobs J_i and J_k.

$NC_{i,k}$ The number of global critical sections entered by J_k and guarded by elements of $\{GS_{i,k}\}$.

Databases

$\mathbf{O}_i$ A database object.

$\mathbf{A}_i$ An atomic data set (ADS). The database is decomposed into disjoint sets called ADS's, and the consistency of each ADS can be maintained independent of other ADS's.

$\mathbf{A}_i[v]$ The version v of an ADS residing in processor i.

$\mathbf{T}_i$ A database transaction.

References

[Ada 83] *Reference Manual for the Ada Programming Language*
U.S. Department of Defense, Washington, D.C., 1983.

[Attar 84] Attar, R., Bernstein P. A. and Goodman N.
Site Initialization, Recovery and Backup in a Distributed Database System.
IEEE Transaction on Software Engineering , Nov., 1984.

[Baker 90] Baker, T. P.
A Stack-Based Resource Allocation Policy for Real-Time Processes.
IEEE Real-Time Systems Symposium , Dec., 1990.

[Beeri 83] Beeri, C., P. A. Bernstein, N. Goodman, and M. Y. Lai.
A Concurrency Control Theory for Nested Transactions.
ACM SIGACT-SIGOPS Symposium on Principles of Distributed Computing , 1983.

[Bernstein 79] Bernstein, Phillip A., David W. Shipman, and Wing S. Wong.
Formal Aspects of Serializability in Database Concurrency Control.
IEEE Transactions on Software Engineering : pages 203 - 216, 1979.

[Borger 89] Borger, M. W. and Rajkumar, R.
Implementing Priority Inheritance Algorithms in an Ada Runtime System.
Technical Report, Software Engineering Institute, Carnegie Mellon University, Pittsburgh, PA, February, 1989.

[Carlow 84] Carlow, G. D.
Architecture of the Space Shuttle Primary Avionics Software System.
Communications of the ACM , September 1984.

[Chen 89]   Chen, M. I. and Lin, K-J.
     Dynamic Priority Ceilings: A Concurrency Control
     Protocol for Real-Time Systems.
     Technical Report, UIUCDCS-R89-1511, Department of
     Computer Science, University of Illinois at Urbana-
     Champaign, 1989.

[Chodrow 91] Chodrow, S., Jahanian, F and Donner, M.
     Run-Time Monitoring of Real-Time Systems.
     Technical Report, IBM T. J. Watson Research Center,
     May, 1991.

[Coffman 83] Coffman Jr., E. G., Garey, M. R. and Johnson, D. S.
     Approximation Algorithms for Bin Packing - An Up-
     dated Survey.
     Technical Report, Bell Laboratories, Murray Hill, N. J.,
     1983.

[Dhall 78]   Dhall, S. K. and Liu, C. L.
     On a Real-Time Scheduling Problem.
     Operations Research, Vol. 26, No. 1, pp. 127-140 ,
     February 1978.

[Dubois 88] Dubois, M., Scheurich, C., Briggs, F. A.
     Synchronization, Coherence and Event Ordering in Mul-
     tiprocessors.
     Computer 21(2):9-21, February, 1988.

[Eswaran 76] Eswaran, K. P., J. N. Gray, R. A. Lorie and I. L. Traiger.
     The Notion of Consistency and Predicate Lock in a
     Database System.
     CACM, Vol. 19, No 11 , Nov. 1976.

[Gait 87]   J. Gait.
     Synchronizing multiprocessor access to shared operating
     system data structures.
     Computer Systems Science and Engineering, Butter-
     worth & Co. 2(4):186-191, October, 1987.

[Garcia-Molina 83]
     Garcia-Molina, H.
     Using Semantic Knowledge For Transaction Processing
     In A Distributed Database.
     ACM Transactions on Database Systems, Vol 8, No. 2 ,
     June, 1983.

163

[Jeffay 89]   Jeffay, K.
                   *Scheduling Sporadic Tasks with Shared Resources in
                   Hard Real-Time Systems.*
                   Technical Report, TR90-038, Department of Computer
                   Science, University of North Carolina at Chapel Hill,
                   November, 1989.

[Kanade 90]   Kanade, T., Mitchell, T., and Whittaker, W.
                   *1989 Year End Report: Autonomous Planetary Rover at
                   Carnegie Mellon.*
                   Technical Report CMU-RI-90-4, Robotics Institute, Car-
                   negie Mellon University, February, 1990.

[Kirk 88]   Kirk, D.
                   Predictable Caches for Real-Time Systems.
                   *Proceedings of the 8th IEEE Real-Time Systems
                   Symposium* , Dec., 1988.

[Lampson 80]   Lampson, B.W., Redell, D.D.
                   Experience with Processes and Monitors in Mesa.
                   Communications of the ACM 23(2):105-117, February,
                   1980.

[Landherr 89]   Landherr, S. F., Klein, M. H.
                   *Inertial Navigation System Simulator: Behavioral
                   Specification.*
                   Technical Report, Software Engineering Institute, Car-
                   negie Mellon University, Pittsburgh, PA, February,
                   1989.

[Lawler 81]   Lawler, E. L.
                   Scheduling Periodically Occurring Tasks on Mul-
                   tiprocessors.
                   Information Processing Letters 12 (1):9 - 12, February,
                   1981.

[Lehoczky 86a]   Lehoczky, J. P. and Sha, L.
                   Performance of Real-Time Bus Scheduling Algorithms.
                   *ACM Performance Evaluation Review, Special Issue Vol.
                   14, No. 1* , May, 1986.

[Lehoczky 86b]   Lehoczky, J. P. and Sha, L.
                   *The Average Case Behavior of The Rate Monotonic
                   Scheduling Algorithm.*
                   Technical Report, Department of Statistics, Carnegie-
                   Mellon University, 1986.

[Lehoczky 87a]   Lehoczky, J. P., Sha, L. and Strosnider, J.
                 Enhancing Aperiodic Responsiveness in A Hard Real-
                     Time Environment.
                 IEEE Real-Time System Symposium , 1987.

[Lehoczky 87b]   Lehoczky, J. P., Sha, L. and Ding, Y.
                 The Rate Monotonic Scheduling Algorithm --- Exact
                     Characterization and Average-Case Behavior.
                 Technical Report, Department of Statistics, Carnegie-
                     Mellon University, 1987.

[Lehoczky 89]   Lehoczky, J. P., Sha, L. and Ding, Y.
                 The Rate Monotonic Scheduling Algorithm --- Exact
                     Characterization and Average-Case Behavior.
                 IEEE Real-Time Systems Symposium , Dec, 1989.

[Leinbaugh 80]   Leinbaugh, D. W.
                 Guaranteed Response Time in a Hard Real-Time En-
                     vironment.
                 IEEE Transactions on Software Engineering , Jan. 1980.

[Leung 80]   Leung, J. Y. and Merrill M. L.
                 A Note on Preemptive Scheduling of Periodic, Real Time
                     Tasks.
                 Information Processing Letters 11 (3):115 - 118, Nov.
                     1980.

[Liu 73]   Liu, C. L. and Layland J. W.
                 Scheduling Algorithms for Multiprogramming in a Hard
                     Real Time Environment.
                 JACM 20 (1):46 - 61, 1973.

[Locke 85]   Jensen, E. D., Locke, C. D. and Tokuda H.
                 A Time-Driven Scheduling Model for Real-time Operat-
                     ing Systems.
                 IEEE Real-Time Systems Symposium , 1985.

[Locke 90]   Locke, C. D., Vogel, D. R., Lucas, L.
                 Generic Avionics Software Specification.
                 Technical Report, Software Engineering Institute, Car-
                     negie Mellon University , 1990.

[Lynch 83]   Lynch, N. A.
                 Multi-level Atomicity - A New Correctness Criterion for
                     Database Concurrency Control.
                 ACM Transactions on Database Systems, Vol. 8, No. 4 ,
                     December, 1983.

[Mohan 86]   Mohan, C., Lindsay, B. and Obermarck R.
Transaction Management in The R* Distributed
  Database Management System.
ACM Transactions on Database Systems, Vol. 11, No. 4 ,
  Dec. 1986.

[Mok 83]   Mok, A. K.
Fundamental Design Problems of Distributed Systems
  For The Hard Real Time Environment.
PhD thesis, M.I.T., 1983.

[Papadimitriou 86]
       Papadimitriou, C.
The Theory of Database Concurrency Control.
Computer Science Press, 1986.

[Rajkumar 87] Rajkumar, R., Sha, L. and Lehoczky, L.
On Countering The Effects of Cycle-Stealing in A Hard
  Real-Time Environment.
IEEE Real-Time Systems Symposium , 1987.

[Rajkumar 88] Rajkumar R., Sha, L., Lehoczky J. P., and Ramam-
ritham, K.
An Optimal Priority Inheritance Protocol for Real-Time
  Synchronization.
Submitted for Publication , 1988.

[Rajkumar 91] Rajkumar, R.
Dealing with Suspending Periodic Tasks.
Submitted for Publication , 1991.

[Ramamritham 84]
       Ramaritham K. and Stankovic J. A.
Dynamic Task Scheduling in Hard Real-Time Dis-
  tributed Systems.
IEEE Software , July, 1984.

[Schwarz 84]   Schwarz, P.
Transactions on Typed Objects.
PhD thesis, Department of Computer Science, Carnegie-
  Mellon University, 1984.

[Sha 86]   Sha, L., Lehoczky, J. P. and Rajkumar, R.
Solutions for Some Practical Problems in Prioritized
  Preemptive Scheduling.
IEEE Real-Time Systems Symposium , 1986.

[Sha 87]   Sha, L., Rajkumar, R. and Lehoczky, J. P.
                Task Scheduling in Distributed Real-Time Systems.
                Proceedings of IEEE Industrial Electronics Conference ,
                    1987.

[Sha 88]   Sha, L., Lehoczky, J. P. and Jensen E. D.
                Modular Concurrency Control and Failure Recovery.
                IEEE Transactions on Computers, Vol. 37, No. 2 , 1988.

[Sha 89]   Sha, L., Rajkumar, R., Lehoczky, J.P., Ramamritham,
                K.
                Mode Changes in a Prioritized Preemptive Scheduling
                    Environment.
                The Real-Time Systems Journal , December, 1989.
                Also available as a Technical Report, Software En-
                    gineering Institute.

[Shatz 87]   Shatz, S.M., Wang, J.,
                Introduction to Distributed Software Engineering.
                Computer 20(10):23-31, Oct, 1987.

[Softech 86]   SofTech, Inc.
                Designing Real-Time Systems in Ada.
                Final Report 1123-1, SofTech, Inc., January, 1986.

[Son 88]   Son, S. H.
                A Message-Based Approach to Distributed Database
                    Prototyping.
                *Fifth IEEE Workshop on Real-Time Software and
                    Operating Systems pp 71-74* , May 1988.

[Sprunt 88]   Brinkley Sprunt, David Kirk, and Lui Sha.
                Priority-Driven, Preemptive I/O Controllers for Real-
                    Time Systems.
                In *Proceedings of the 15th International Symposium on
                    Computer Architecture*, pages 152-159. IEEE,
                    Honolulu, Hawaii, June, 1988.

[Sprunt 89]   Sprunt, H.M.B., Sha, L., and Lehoczky, J.P.
                Aperiodic Task Scheduling on Hard Real-Time Systems.
                The Real-Time Systems Journal , June, 1989.

[Stankovic 88] John A. Stankovic.
                Misconceptions about Real-Time Computing.
                Computer 21(10):10-19, Oct., 1988.

[Stone 77]   Stone, H.S.
Multiprocessor Scheduling with the Aid of Network
    Flow Algorithms.
IEEE Trans. Software Engineering :85-93, Jan, 1977.

[Strosnider 88]   Strosnider, J.K.
Highly Responsive Real-Time Token Rings.
PhD thesis, Carnegie Mellon University, August, 1988.

[Weihl 83]   Weihl, W. E. and Liskov, B.
Specification and Implementation of Resilient Atomic
    Data Types.
*Proceedings of The SIGPLAN Symposium on Program-
    ming Language Issues* , June, 1983.

[Wellings 88]   Wellings, A. J.
Distributed Execution - Units of Partitioning: Session
    Summary.
*The 2nd International Workshop on Real-Time Ada
    Issues* :80-85, June, 1988.

[Zhao 87a]   Zhao, W., Ramamritham, K. and Stankovic, J.
Preemptive Scheduling Under Time and Resource Con-
    straints.
IEEE Transactions on Computers , Aug. 1987.

[Zhao 87b]   Zhao, W., Ramamritham, K., and Stankovic, J. A.
Scheduling Tasks with Resource Requirements in Hard
    Real-Time Systems.
IEEE Transactions on Software Engineering , May 1987.

Index